YORK NOTES

D0552978

OF MICE AND MEN

JOHN STEINBECK

NOTES BY MARTIN STEPHEN

 Longman

York Press

YORK PRESS
322 Old Brompton Road, London SW5 9JH

PEARSON EDUCATION LIMITED
Edinburgh Gate, Harlow,
Essex CM20 2JE, United Kingdom
Associated companies, branches and representatives throughout the world

First published 1997
This new and fully revised edition first published 2002
Third impression 2003

10 9 8 7 6 5 4 3

ISBN 0-582-50622-0

Designed by Michelle Cannatella
Phototypeset by Gem Graphics, Trenance, Mawgan Porth, Cornwall
Colour reproduction and film output by Spectrum Colour
Produced by Pearson Education Asia Limited, Hong Kong

CONTENTS

PREFACE

York Notes are designed to give you a broader perspective on works of literature studied at GCSE and equivalent levels. With examination requirements changing in the twenty-first century, we have made a number of significant changes to this new series. We continue to help students to reach their own interpretations of the text but York Notes now have important extra-value new features.

You will discover that York Notes are genuinely interactive. The new **Checkpoint** features make sure that you can test your knowledge and broaden your understanding. You will also be directed to excellent websites, books and films where you can follow up ideas for yourself.

The **Resources** section has been updated and an entirely new section has been devoted to how to improve your grade. Careful reading and application of the principles laid out in the Resources section guarantee improved performance.

The **Detailed summaries** include an easy-to-follow skeleton structure of the story-line, while the section on **Language and style** has been extended to offer an in-depth discussion of the writer's techniques.

The Contents page shows the structure of this study guide. However, there is no need to read from the beginning to the end as you would with a novel, play or poem. Use the Notes in the way that suits you. Our aim is to help you with your understanding of the work, not to dictate how you should learn.

Our authors are practising English teachers and examiners who have used their experience to offer a whole range of **Examiner's secrets** – useful hints to encourage exam success.

The General Editor of this series is John Polley, Senior GCSE Examiner and former Head of English at Harrow Way Community School, Andover.

The author of these Notes is Dr Martin Stephen, High Master of Manchester Grammar School and ex-Head of The Perse School, Cambridge. Educated at the Universities of Leeds and Sheffield, he is the author of sixteen academic books and two novels.

The text used in these Notes is the Penguin paperback edition, published in 2000.

PART ONE

INTRODUCTION

HOW TO STUDY A NOVEL

A novelist starts with a story that examines a situation and the actions of particular characters. Remember that authors are not photographers, and that a novel never resembles real life exactly. Ultimately, a novel represents a view of the world that has been created in the author's imagination.

There are six features of a novel:

❶ THE STORY: this is the series of events, deliberately organised by the writer to test the characters

❷ THE CHARACTERS: the people who have to respond to the events of the story. Since they are human, they can be good or bad, clever or stupid, likeable or detestable, etc. They may change too!

❸ THE VIEWPOINT/VOICE: who is telling the story. The viewpoint may come from one of the characters, or from an omniscient (all-seeing) narrator, which allows the novelist to write about the perspectives of all the characters

❹ THE THEMES: these are the underlying messages, or meanings, of the novel

❺ THE SETTING: this concerns the time and place that the author has chosen for the story

❻ THE LANGUAGE AND STYLE: these are the words that the author has used to influence our understanding of the novel

To arrive at the fullest understanding of a novel, you need to read it several times. In this way, you can see how all the choices the author has made add up to a particular view of life, and develop your own ideas about it.

The purpose of these York Notes is to help you understand what the novel is about and to enable you to make your own interpretation. Do not expect the study of a novel to be neat and easy: novels are chosen for examination purposes, not written for them!

DID YOU KNOW?

Steinbeck's stage-play version of *Of Mice and Men* won the prize for Best New York Play.

AUTHOR – LIFE AND WORKS

1912 John Ernst Steinbeck born 27 February in Salinas, California

1919 Attends Stanford University

1925 Leaves university for New York without taking a degree

1929 Publishes *Cup of Gold*

1930 Marries Carol Henning

1932 *Pastures of Heaven* published

1933 *To a God Unknown* published

1935 First successful novel, *Tortilla Flat*, published

1937 *Of Mice and Men* published

1939 Publishes *The Grapes of Wrath*

1940 Marriage breaks up when he meets Gwendolyn Conger; *Grapes of Wrath* wins Pulitzer Prize

1942 Marries Gwendolyn Conger

1944 *Cannery Row* published

1947 *The Pearl* published

1948 Divorces Gwendolyn Conger

1950 Marries Elaine Scott

1952 *East of Eden* published

1955 Settles in Sag Harbor, Long Island

1961 *The Winter of Our Discontent* published

1962 Awarded Nobel Prize for Literature

1968 Dies of heart disease 20 December, aged 66

CONTEXT

1901 Theodore Roosevelt elected as president

1917 USA enters First World War

1918 War ends

1919 Prohibition commences

1929 'Great Crash' on Wall Street, spelling start of Great Depression

1932 Stock market falls to lowest point

1933 Franklin D. Roosevelt elected as president

1939–45 Second World War in Europe

1941 Japan attacks Pearl Harbor; USA enters Second World War

1945 First atomic bombs exploded over Hiroshima and Nagasaki

1950–53 Korean War

1954 Supreme Court rules racial segregation in schools unconstitutional

1961 John F. Kennedy elected president

1963 John F. Kennedy assassinated

1964 Civil Rights Act enacted

1965 USA begins military support for Vietnam

SETTING AND BACKGROUND

JOHN STEINBECK'S BACKGROUND

Early days

John Ernst Steinbeck was born on 27 February 1902, in Salinas, California, USA. The Salinas River is mentioned in the first line of *Of Mice and Men*. The whole novel is centred on the landscape around Salinas. Steinbeck was the third of four children, of mixed German and Irish descent. His parents owned a considerable amount of land, and his mother was a schoolteacher who encouraged him to read widely. His background was neither rich nor poor, and his parents wanted him to follow a 'respectable' career.

Graduation

Steinbeck left Salinas High School in 1919. He wrote some pieces for his school magazine, but showed no real signs of the great writer he was to become in his adult life. (Take heart if you think you have the ability to be a great novelist!) He went on to Stanford University to study Marine Biology, but in order to finance his studies had to take long periods away from university, working to earn money. His jobs included clerk, shop assistant, waiter and labourer, as well as 'breaking army remounts for officers' gentle behinds'. This meant taking the semi-wild horses bought by the US Army and rendering them fit to be ridden by officers. Throughout his life Steinbeck

CHECKPOINT 1

Steinbeck loved horses and dogs, though there is only one live animal that plays any real part in the novel. Whose is it?

revealed a deep love of horses and dogs. Interestingly for anyone who reads *Of Mice and Men*, one of his jobs was as a ranch hand near King City. It was this experience he drew on most closely in writing the novel.

Taking a risk

Steinbeck challenged his family and its values in order to be a creative writer. He left university in 1925 without taking a degree and went to New York. His parents wanted him to be a lawyer, a 'respectable' career. Steinbeck wanted to be a writer. For ten years it seemed as if they were right and he was wrong. He was sacked as a reporter, left New York and took on a succession of temporary jobs.

Even to get to New York he had had to work his passage as a seaman aboard a freighter. His other jobs included work as a caretaker, a mail coach driver and work in the local fish hatchery, Cannery Row near Monterey. There he met his first wife, Carol Henning. She had come to the fish hatchery as a tourist and met Steinbeck first of all as her guide. Steinbeck moved to San Francisco, where Carol had a job. They married in 1930.

Success

A key figure in Steinbeck's success was his father. He supported his son through the bleak years when he was trying to establish himself, giving him an allowance and letting Steinbeck and his wife live in the family's holiday home rent-free. Outwardly there was little to justify his belief in his son. Steinbeck's first novel, *Cup of Gold*, was rejected several times before finding a publisher in 1929, and even then it failed financially.

Steinbeck's literary agents, McIntosh and Otis, agreed to take him on and promote his work in 1931. They were crucial in his success, because they kept faith in him when no one else seemed to believe he had a future as a writer. Steinbeck was loyal to his friends. In 1962, when he was awarded the Nobel Prize for Literature, he insisted that McIntosh and Otis take a percentage of the very considerable prize money, just as if the award had been a contract they had obtained for him.

DID YOU KNOW?

Steinbeck's temporary jobs were a desperate necessity to keep him alive, but provided huge amounts of information for his later novels.

CHECK THE BOOK

Steinbeck's novel *Cannery Row* is based on his experience working at Cannery Row in Monterey.

It took until 1935 for Steinbeck to achieve his first real publishing success. In the ten years since he had left university without a degree, America had suffered a savage recession, hitting book sales hard.

Steinbeck's second novel, *Pastures of Heaven* (1932) and his third, *To A God Unknown* (1933) were published by firms on the edge of bankruptcy. Amidst all this uncertainty, Steinbeck had to face the protracted and agonising illnesses of both his parents. His paralysed mother hung on for a year before finally dying in 1934. But his father meant more to Steinbeck. He died in 1936, and for his last two or three years was a desperately unhappy and senile old man, physically incapable and mentally stagnant.

However, not long afterwards, success came with *Tortilla Flat* (1935) and *Of Mice and Men* (1937). Both were commercially successful, and both were eventually made into films. *Of Mice and Men* was turned into a play and won a Drama Critics award. It was also made the monthly selection of the Book of the Month Club, which guaranteed huge sales for it. Steinbeck used some of the money to finance a trip he made with migrant workers in California.

This experience was to become the basis of what is probably still his best-known novel, *The Grapes of Wrath* (1939). It is one of the greatest novels to have come out of the United States in the twentieth century. Before its publication, Steinbeck wrote to the publishers suggesting they only printed a few copies, as he did not think it would be successful!

Steinbeck the man

Steinbeck was married three times and divorced twice. His first marriage to Carol Henning fell apart in 1940, when he met a professional singer called Gwendolyn Conger in Hollywood. He married her in 1942, produced two sons but was divorced again by 1948 on the grounds of incompatibility. He said of his first marriage that it was the story of two people who hurt each other for eleven years, but he never lost touch completely with his first wife. His third marriage, to Elaine Scott in 1950, brought him his greatest happiness in a relationship.

Financial success was welcome, but Steinbeck found it hard to cope

CHECK THE NET
You can have a visual tour of Steinbeck's homes at Pacific Grove on 'John Steinbecks' Pacific Grove' web site. Find it on **www.93950.com**

CHECK THE BOOK
Get a copy of the text for the play *Of Mice and Men* from a library and compare it with the novel. What has been left out from the novel and what has been added on, and what does this tell you about the different style required for plays and novels?

with being famous. He moved in high circles in his later years, developing warm relationships with no less than three American presidents – Theodore Roosevelt, Lyndon B. Johnson and John F. Kennedy – but wrote only three books in this period that are still widely read today, *Cannery Row* (1944), *East of Eden* (1952) and *The Winter of Our Discontent* (1961). He was awarded the Nobel Prize for Literature in 1962, one of the greatest literary honours an author can receive. Steinbeck died in 1968 of heart disease. He was buried in Salinas, California, a last return to the setting for *Of Mice and Men*.

 DID YOU KNOW?
Steinbeck has been damned by right-wing conservatives for being a revolutionary and by left-wing figures for *not* being a revolutionary!

Steinbeck was a lonely, modest and restless man. He was never content and always searching for something more. He was a difficult man to live with, yet an easy one to love, something he shares with many great writers and artists. His love of the outdoors, of animals and of individual human beings shines through in *Of Mice and Men*.

MIGRANT FARM WORKERS

George and Lennie are examples of the 'migrant' or 'itinerant' farm workers who fuelled and made possible the intensive farming economy. These men would travel great distances, either walking, using cheap bus services, hitch-hiking or travelling by train in the empty boxcars that were later used to ship out the grain they helped to farm. They would receive $2.50 or $3.00 a day, plus board (food) and a room. The food was basic, the room sometimes nothing more than a shared tent, but industrial action at the time of the First World War (1914–1918) had increased wages alongside an increase in the price of grain. Yet this whole lifestyle was being threatened by drastic changes that were affecting America. Not long before the time in which *Of Mice and Men* is set 350 men would be needed to complete a major harvest. By the time it was written half the available work was being done by machinery which required only five men to work it.

Before the days of mechanisation the mule driver was at the top of the social tree. A good mule driver could control a line of up to twenty mules single-handedly. Such a driver was regarded highly by the farm owner, who recognised how much work he could do and how much money he could save, but also respected by the farm workers themselves for his skill. Slim is just such a figure in *Of Mice*

and Men. The reward for his skill is that he has permanent
employment on the farm. Had he chosen to move, his skill could
have commanded a high wage.

THE AMERICAN DREAM

Many farm workers would share George and Lennie's dream of a
smallholding or small farm. Such an acquisition would allow men
such as George to be their own masters, and to make a decent, if
unspectacular, living from the sweat of their own brows. Such a
dream is one part of the much larger phenomenon known as the
American Dream.

The American Dream arose from the way in which America was first
populated. Its people came from almost every country and
background, but were united by a belief that America would give
them the opportunities denied them in their present country. Those
who came to live in America were driven by hope of a new life. For
some, the lure was political or religious freedom from persecution.
For very many others, America offered escape from grinding poverty
or starvation. It was a new country and an undiscovered one. In
Europe, land had always been the key to financial independence and
status. Only in America could the poor of Europe hope to settle
virgin farmland. The frontier was expanding, gold fields were being

**EXAMINER'S
SECRET**
Examiners want you
to study a novel
within its historical
context. How much
is *Of Mice and Men*
affected by the
times in which its
author lived? How
much is it a novel
about those times?

discovered daily and waiting to be mined, and mass immigration was presenting every possible opportunity for money, careers and reputations to be made.

DID YOU KNOW?

The National Steinbeck Center may be found in Salinas, the setting for *Of Mice and Men*.

The American Dream was the popular idea that America was a country that allowed men and women to make a clean start, to achieve prosperity and security. The reality did not always match the dream. The destruction of the Native American 'Red Indian' population, the appalling horror of the American Civil War, the creation of ecologically disastrous urban and industrial slums, and the corruption of many city managers were all growing pains of a new and great country. Yet the dream survived for a long time.

Death of a dream

The American Dream survived until the late 1920s. By then there was no more frontier, no more virgin land to be claimed and America had built its own aristocracy on the basis of wealth and its own system of repression based on race.

DID YOU KNOW?

When there was no more frontier and no more Red Indians to fight, 'Wild West' shows toured the cities of America and Europe, presenting a highly glamorised version of life on the frontier.

The final blow was dealt by the Wall Street Crash, when the bottom fell out of the stock market and share prices. This marked the start of the Great Depression that was to sweep the whole world in the 1930s. Farming was as badly affected as any other area of the economy. Decay there was sped up by the fact that ignorance and over-farming had resulted in hundreds of thousands of acres of farmland drying up, losing their precious top soil and being turned into little more than desert. This was the creation of the famous 'dust bowl'. Poor crops meant that many of the farmers were unable to pay back the debts they had taken out in order to buy the land in the first place.

Thus the way of life of men such as George, Lennie and Slim was coming to an end when *Of Mice and Men* was written, pushed by the twin forces of mechanisation and economic recession. George and Lennie's world was becoming history. Their dream of freedom and independence was probably doomed before they acquired it. Lennie makes George recite their dream to him at the end of the novel, not realising that George is preparing to shoot him before he is lynched by the pursuing mob. Lennie dies at George's hands, in an act of mercy. The dream they and many other migrant workers shared – 'We gonna get a little place' – is as doomed as Lennie.

ORDINARY PEOPLE

All the trends and events mentioned above had happened or were happening by the time *Of Mice and Men* was written. Is it therefore a novel about the end of the American Dream, about social change and about the exploitation of itinerant workers? Steinbeck knew about the changes. He cared about them. Yet the probable answer is that *Of Mice and Men* is a book about people, and a book which cares about people. Steinbeck does little probing of the reasons behind social problems. He is concerned simply with looking at them as they are.

Do a simple test after reading *Of Mice and Men*. Would you have known about the Great Depression, the creation of the 'dust bowl' and the increasing mechanisation of farming unless you had read a guide such as this? The answer is probably not. This knowledge helps you to understand the book. It does not explain it.

SALINAS

The countryside Steinbeck knew and loved is the background to the novel. The foreground is occupied by people who are human enough to have come from any area or region. This is not a novel about Salinas. It is a novel with Salinas in it.

CHECKPOINT 2

Do you think George knows that he and Lennie will never achieve their dream, and that they are doomed?

 CHECK THE FILM

All the films made of *Of Mice and Men* have focused on the beauty of the landscape and the wide, open spaces of Salinas and its region.

Now take a break!

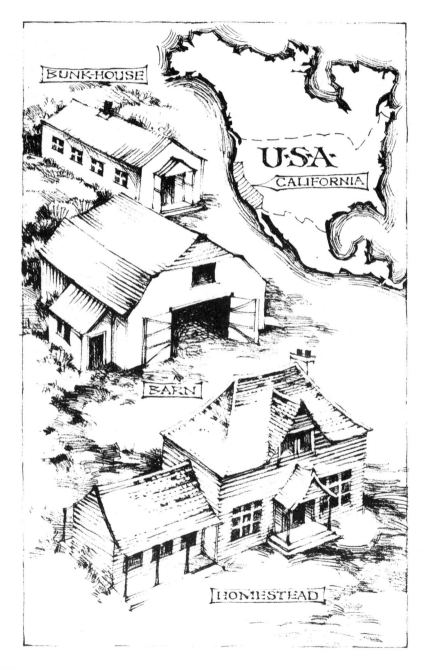

BUNK-HOUSE

U·S·A·
CALIFORNIA

BARN

HOMESTEAD

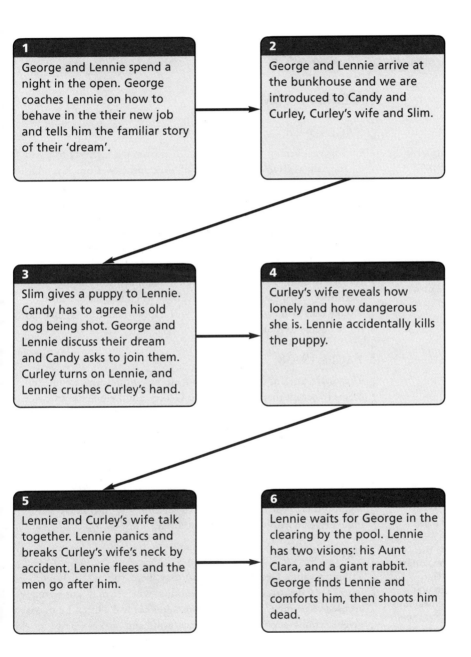

1
George and Lennie spend a night in the open. George coaches Lennie on how to behave in the their new job and tells him the familiar story of their 'dream'.

2
George and Lennie arrive at the bunkhouse and we are introduced to Candy and Curley, Curley's wife and Slim.

3
Slim gives a puppy to Lennie. Candy has to agree his old dog being shot. George and Lennie discuss their dream and Candy asks to join them. Curley turns on Lennie, and Lennie crushes Curley's hand.

4
Curley's wife reveals how lonely and how dangerous she is. Lennie accidentally kills the puppy.

5
Lennie and Curley's wife talk together. Lennie panics and breaks Curley's wife's neck by accident. Lennie flees and the men go after him.

6
Lennie waits for George in the clearing by the pool. Lennie has two visions: his Aunt Clara, and a giant rabbit. George finds Lennie and comforts him, then shoots him dead.

PART TWO

SUMMARIES

GENERAL SUMMARY

PAGES 3–18

DID YOU KNOW?

When there was no work, farm workers such as George and Lennie had to try and earn enough money over the summer to keep themselves alive over the whole winter.

One warm evening two men walk down from the highway to a pool by the Salinas River. George is small, dark and moves quickly, whilst it soon becomes apparent that Lennie, huge and blank-faced, is simple-minded. They are off to take up work on a nearby ranch, but George tells Lennie not to say a word when they arrive; they have had to leave their previous job for some unspecified reason to do with Lennie. Lennie angers George by showing that he has kept a dead mouse to stroke its fur. George makes Lennie throw it away. Before they go to sleep, Lennie gets George to tell him a story he has obviously heard many times before, how when they have a little money they will run a small farm, with rabbits and other animals on it for Lennie to look after.

PAGES 19–38

They start work at the farm. The ranch owner questions Lennie but seems to accept that he is harmless. George and Lennie meet Curley, the violent, aggressive and argumentative son of the ranch owner. He has recently married a girl who is showing signs of wanting to be unfaithful to him. She comes into the bunk-house and flaunts herself. Lennie is attracted to her, and George becomes worried. Frightened that there will be trouble between Curley and Lennie, George arranges to meet Lennie by the pool where they spent the previous night, if there is any trouble. They meet Slim, the chief horse and mule driver, a man with natural authority.

PAGES 39–65

CHECK THE FILM

Some critics feel that the Lewis Milestone 1939 film was about the Depression, whilst the 1992 Gary Sinese film was about friendship. How can the same story seem to be treated so differently in films?

Talking to Slim, George reveals that they were 'run out' of Weed, where they had previously been working, when Lennie was wrongly accused of trying to rape a girl. Slim's dog has had a litter. Lennie is given a young puppy, and Carlson, a farm hand, makes Candy, an old man who cleans up round the farm, let his aged dog be shot. It smells and is too old to be of any further use. Depressed by the loss of his dog, Candy hears George telling Lennie about their plans for a little farm, and offers to put up over half the money if they will let him come in with them. George finally begins to believe that his dream will become a reality. Curley breaks in, and starts a fight with Lennie. After taking a battering, Lennie crushes Curley's hand when George orders him to fight back. Slim makes Curley say that his hand was injured in an accident with a machine.

PAGES 66–82

One evening when nearly everyone has gone out to the local town, Lennie enters Crooks's hut. Crooks is a crippled and embittered black man who works on the farm in the stables. Lennie and Candy tell Crooks about their plan for a farm, but they are interrupted by Curley's wife, who threatens Crooks with a false rape charge when she is asked to leave the hut. Later Lennie kills the pup he has been given, not knowing his own strength.

EXAMINER'S SECRET

Examiners don't like it when a student simply repeats the story of the novel!

PAGES 83–97

While Lennie is trying to bury the puppy in the straw on the barn floor, Curley's wife comes in. They talk, and she asks him to stroke her hair. She panics when she feels Lennie's strength and by accident Lennie breaks her neck. When the body is found it is obvious that Lennie is the murderer. A hunt is started for him.

PAGES 98–106

George realises that Lennie could not bear life in prison, and cannot bear seeing him lynched by the farm hands who are hunting him. He goes to where he knows Lennie will be, and shoots him. Only Slim understands why he had to do this.

CHECKPOINT 3

Does the presence of Crooks make this a novel about racism? Or is it simply about everyone who is crushed by society?

DETAILED SUMMARIES

PAGES 3–18 – Moving on

EXAMINER'S SECRET

When an exam asks you to comment on an extract from the novel, examiners often choose the opening or closing sections!

❶ George and Lennie spend a night in the open.

❷ George coaches Lennie on how to behave in the their new job.

❸ George throws away the dead mouse Lennie has been petting.

❹ We learn that accusations in Weed forced George and Lennie to flee.

❺ George tells Lennie the familiar story of their 'dream'.

The book opens with a description of the country around the Salinas River, south of Soledad in California. Look how many different colours (green, yellow, gold and white) and how many different animals (lizard, racoon, rabbit, dog and deer) are mentioned in the first, short paragraph. Steinbeck has a very powerful descriptive style. Look how detailed it is: it is the 'lower leaf junctures' that are green, and he even notes that the deer's tracks are 'split-wedge' (p. 3).

CHECKPOINT 4

Identify the animals that Lennie is likened to in the novel.

We are introduced to the main characters, George and Lennie, as they come down from the highway to a pool by the river. George is small and dark, Lennie huge and ponderous. Lennie is described by comparing him to a variety of animals: We call such descriptions **similes**. What effect do they have on us? Some readers think it is a mistake to describe Lennie as a 'like a terrier' (p. 10), as these dogs are small creatures and he is so huge. Others argue that the relationship between George and Lennie is like that between a master and his dog.

DID YOU KNOW?

The fact that the water Lennie drinks from at the start of the novel is described by George as 'kinda scummy' (p. 5) is said by some critics to warn us of an unhappy ending.

Lennie drinks from the stagnant water of the pool and is told off for so doing by George. Note Steinbeck's use of **dialogue**. The two characters give us information about what they think and about their personalities by how they talk. The two men are heading for work on a nearby ranch, but have been dropped short of their destination by a bus driver. It is obvious that Lennie is simple, and George makes him get rid of a dead mouse that he has been petting in his pocket. Lennie loves to pet mice, but kills them when he does so. This is a clear

CHECK THE FILM

Many films have emulated the pairing of George and Lennie. Watch *Rain Man* (1988), for instance, and look at the relationship between Raymond and Charlie.

warning about how dangerous Lennie can be. Does his innocence and his unawareness of the threat he poses make him more or less menacing?

Before the two men settle down to share three cans of beans for supper, George gives Lennie strict instructions not to say anything when they meet the boss of the ranch the next day, because if Lennie does speak the boss will realise 'what a crazy bastard' (p. 8) he is. George has decided to spend the night in the open. Lennie asks why they do not go straight to the ranch, where there will be food. George says it is because they are starting hard work tomorrow, and he wants to savour the freedom of sleeping out in the open. George sends Lennie off to get wood for a cooking fire. When he returns George spots that Lennie has retrieved the dead mouse. George takes it from Lennie, who does not want to give it up, and throws it as far away as he can, because it is no longer 'fresh' (p. 11).

Steinbeck withholds information from us to build up suspense and interest. We know that something went wrong in Weed; we have to wait to find out what it was. It emerges that in Weed, where they were previously working, Lennie stroked the material of a girl's dress. She was frightened and tried to break away. Lennie clung on and the girl accused Lennie of trying to rape her. George and Lennie had to hide in an irrigation ditch and flee the town. George gets angry with

GLOSSARY

junctures where one or more things (here, branches) join together

Lennie, firstly because looking after Lennie limits George so much in what he can do, and secondly because Lennie keeps on getting both of them into trouble. Lennie is very hurt, and offers to leave and go and live in a cave. He also plays cleverly on George's guilt at having thrown away the mouse.

CHECKPOINT 5

Lennie is shown to have attacked a girl at the start of the novel and he kills one at the end. How is it that he still appears as a 'gentle giant'?

George and Lennie's dream

George relents, and as the sun sets he tells Lennie a story they have obviously been through very many times, so many that Lennie knows part of it off by heart. It is their dream, about how they are going to buy a few acres of land, raise their own animals and live an independent and happy existence. They will have rabbits on the farm, and Lennie will be allowed to tend these and all the other animals. Comforted by the repetition of their dream, they go to sleep.

Warm colours and soft sounds combine to create an air of peace and contentment in this first section. Yet right at the end of the book the water-snake that was swimming peacefully in the river at the start of the novel is plucked out and eaten by a heron. Steinbeck uses this **image** to warn us that nature combines peace and violence, with sudden swings from one to the other. We must therefore expect something similar for the humans who live so closely in this world.

WHO SAYS ...?

1 'If he finds out what a crazy bastard you are, we won't get no job'

....

5 'Someday – we're gonna get the jack together and we're gonna have a little house and a couple of acres an' a cow and some pigs'

....

2 'They run us outta Weed'

....

4 'God a'mighty, if I was alone I could live so easy.'

....

3 'I'd pet 'em, and pretty soon they bit my fingers and I pinched their heads a little and then they was dead – because they was so little.'

....

ABOUT WHOM?

6 'Wonder he isn't too damn good to stop in Soledad at all.'

....

7 'Lady, huh? Don't even remember who that lady was.'

....

Check your answers on p. 70.

PAGES 19-38 – Rising tensions

1 We are shown the bunkhouse and introduced to Candy and Curley.

2 Curley and Lennie have an argument.

3 Curley's wife visits the bunkhouse, and George becomes even more worried.

4 We meet Slim, the leader of the farm hands.

CHECK THE FILM

Some critics think that the actors who played George, Lennie and Curley's wife were poor performances or bad casting in the 1992 Gary Sinese film. See what you think!

This section introduces us to the main characters at the ranch. Again, **characterisation** is undertaken through **dialogue**. Each character has their own different way of speaking – look at sentence length, use of slang, repetition and accents. The characters are all ranch-hands or work on the same farm, but immediately we meet them we see how different they are, from the dignity of Slim to the anger of Curley.

CHECKPOINT 6

What do we learn about the bunkhouse from the opening paragraph of this section?

Candy, the old man who cleans out the farm buildings, shows George and Lennie the bunkhouse. Candy lost his hand whilst working on the farm, and was allowed to stay on in this lowly position as cleaner. Characterisation is also achieved through other methods. Candy's dog is old and physically infirm, with nothing to look forward to except death. Is the owner, Candy, being characterised at the same time as his dog, by association?

George is worried in case the last occupier of the bunk left it infested with lice, but is reassured by Candy. George's concern about the cleanliness of his bunk helps to suggest that he is a 'clean', decent man. The description of George putting his few possessions on to the shelves round his bunk is somehow pathetic, revealing how little such men have that is their own, and how rootless their life is.

George and Lennie meet the boss of the ranch, quite a reasonable man whose only real weakness seems to be that when he is in a bad mood he loses his temper with the black man who runs the farm stable. He is suspicious of George and Lennie, but is eventually satisfied that they will do good work for him.

> **CHECKPOINT 7**
> How is George's physical and mental cleanliness emphasised in this section?

Curley

Curley, the boss's son, comes into the bunk-house looking for his father. Curley is an ex-lightweight boxer who is always picking fights with people, and who seems to have a particular grudge against people bigger than himself: the swamper tells us that 'He hates big guys' (p. 28). We see this in Curley's attitude towards Lennie.

Most of what we hear about Curley comes from the mouth of the swamper, and he is shown as thoroughly dangerous and foul. He claims to keep a glove on one hand full of Vaseline (a lubricating petroleum jelly), to improve his sexual performance. This is another example of a physical **image** that describes the mentality of the character.

DID YOU KNOW?
Blue jeans, which are now designer fashion items, were developed in America as cheap and durable work trousers.

We are told that Curley is very concerned about his wife, whom he married a fortnight ago, because she is giving all the men on the ranch 'the eye' (p. 29), suggesting she wants to sleep with them. Curley almost immediately picks an argument with Lennie. George is convinced that there will be trouble between Curley and Lennie. He warns Lennie to meet back where they camped the previous night if there is any trouble.

When Curley comes into the bunk-house again, looking for his wife, there is an immediate increase in tension and George becomes even more worried.

After Curley's wife has been described by the swamper, she comes into the bunkhouse. When Steinbeck talks of Curley's wife's hair as being, 'in little rolled clusters, like sausages' (p. 32), we see his skill for unusual and therefore vivid descriptive language. Curley's wife uses the excuse that she is looking for Curley, but does not seem to want to leave. Lennie is fascinated by her and George tries to warn him off.

George and Lennie then meet Slim, the 'jerkline skinner' (p. 34). Slim is a man of great dignity and natural authority. Slim is intrigued by George and Lennie going around together. He points out how rare this is, and how lonely and isolated most migrant ranch workers are.

The pair also meet Carlson, a ranch hand. Carlson reveals that Slim's dog has had a litter of puppies. He suggests that Slim might give one of the pups to Candy, whose old dog is infirm and stinks out the bunkhouse. Lennie becomes highly excited at the possibility of being given one of the puppies himself.

Now take a break!

WHO SAYS ...?

1 'You seen a girl around here?'
....

5 'This ain't no good place. I wanna get outta here.'
....

2 'A guy on a ranch don't never listen nor he don't ast no questions.'
....

4 'Ain't many guys travel around together,' he mused. 'I don't know why. Maybe ever'body in the whole damn world is scared of each other.'
....

3 'That dog of Candy's is so God damn old he can't hardly walk. Stinks like hell, too.'
....

ABOUT WHOM?

6 'Well, he's a pretty nice fella. Gets pretty mad sometimes, but he's pretty nice'
....

8 There was a gravity in his manner and a quiet so profound that all talk stopped when he spoke. His authority was so great that his word was taken on any subject, be it politics or love.
....

7 'He hates big guys. He's alla time picking scraps with big guys.'
....

Check your answers on p. 70.

PAGES 39–65 – The dawn of hope

DID YOU KNOW?

When Steinbeck was writing *East of Eden* in his special writing room in his New York house, he also built a boat there on a carpenter's work bench he had had installed.

❶ Slim gives a puppy to Lennie.

❷ Slim and George talk about Lennie.

❸ Candy has to agree to his old dog being shot.

❹ George and Lennie discuss their dream and Candy asks to join them.

❺ Slim and Curley argue over Curley's wife.

❻ When Curley turns on Lennie, Lennie first of all does nothing.

❼ George orders Lennie to defend himself and Lennie crushes Curley's hand.

❽ Slim protects Lennie from blame for the injury to Curley.

CHECKPOINT 8

How much of the novel is written in **dialogue**, and how much does Steinbeck allow the reader to find out about the characters by letting them speak out loud to us?

It is evening in the bunkhouse. Slim has given a puppy to Lennie, and he and George talk. George feels able to tell Slim why he looks after Lennie. They were brought up in the same town, and when Lennie's Aunt Clara died, Lennie came out to work with George. George says that he just got used to working with Lennie, and things developed from there. He admits that early on, being with Lennie made him feel superior, and made him order Lennie to do stupid things so that he could show off the authority he had over Lennie and laugh at him. He now realises how bad this was. So why does George stay with Lennie? The answer is given partly by George, whose comments reveal the utter loneliness of the life of an itinerant farm hand.

Note the importance that light plays in Steinbeck's description. Much of the atmosphere in the discussion between Slim and George is created by the pool of light that the shaded lamp throws in the bunkhouse.

Lennie tries to take his puppy to bed with him, but is stopped by George. Carlson cannot stand the smell of Candy's old dog and asks Slim to give Candy one of the pups so that the old dog can be shot. The decision is postponed briefly when a young ranch hand shows Slim a letter in one of the western magazines that the hands love to read, written by a hand who used to work at the ranch. The ranch hands outwardly scorn the Wild West magazines that they buy, but secretly they lap up the romanticised, glamorous view they give of cowboys and, by association, of ranch hands. The magazines show the workers how they would like to be. This is another dream, similar to that of George and Lennie. It will never be real, but it is necessary for surviving in the real world. An unwilling Candy allows Carlson to take away his dog and shoot it. He is deeply upset.

CHECKPOINT 9

George tells Slim how they came to be chased out of Weed. What new information do we get about this?

George and Whit, another ranch hand, talk about Curley's wife and about Susy's, a local brothel where the men go on Saturday nights. Note how delicately Steinbeck handles the discussion. It could easily become coarse and obscene. In Steinbeck's hands it becomes natural, a normal part of a man's life. This is not to justify the use of prostitutes, but it shows how Steinbeck refuses to impose a politically-correct agenda on to his writing. Steinbeck is concerned to reveal what the men think and feel, not to prove a point about what they ought to think. As the two men talk, Curley bursts in and, seeing Slim is not there, rushes out thinking Slim is with his wife.

Lennie comes in and he and George start dreaming out loud about the little farm they are going to buy. Candy asks if such a farm actually exists. George says that he knows one owned by old people who might be willing to sell for $600 or so. Candy confesses he has

CHECKPOINT 10

What modern magazines are the equivalent of the ranch-hands' cowboy magazines?

CHECKPOINT 11

Do we really ever believe that George and Lennie will achieve their dream? Check up on how many hints are given that there will be a tragic ending to the book.

 CHECK THE FILM

There is an excellent profile of John Steinbeck on video, entitled *Famous Authors: John Steinbeck*, widely available from any good video outlet.

$350 saved up and asks if he can come in with them. For the first time George really begins to believe that his dream might become a reality. All he needs to do is work for another month or two and not spend anything and they will have the stake to buy the farm.

The mood is shattered when Slim and Curley burst in, Slim furious at being falsely accused by Curley over his wife. Curley turns on Lennie, and attacks him viciously. The episode is carefully timed to shatter the dream-vision that George, Lennie and Candy have built up. It is the heron killing the water-snake (see p. 98), a reminder that dreams can exist for only a short while in the real world. It is also a reminder that the world can be violent, cruel and unforgiving. At first Lennie does nothing, but when ordered to fight back by George, he crushes Curley's hand. There is hardly a bone in the hand that is not broken, but before Curley goes off to hospital, Slim makes him promise to say that his hand was damaged in a machine, thus diverting any blame from Lennie.

Now take a break!

WHO SAYS ...?

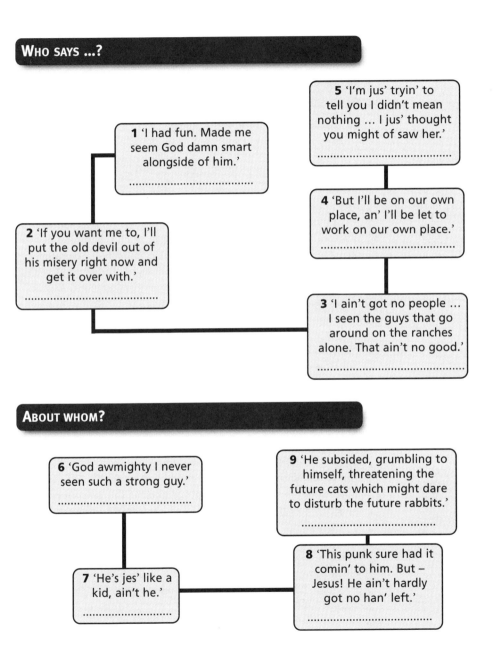

1 'I had fun. Made me seem God damn smart alongside of him.'

....

2 'If you want me to, I'll put the old devil out of his misery right now and get it over with.'

....

5 'I'm jus' tryin' to tell you I didn't mean nothing ... I jus' thought you might of saw her.'

....

4 'But I'll be on our own place, an' I'll be let to work on our own place.'

....

3 'I ain't got no people ... I seen the guys that go around on the ranches alone. That ain't no good.'

....

ABOUT WHOM?

6 'God awmighty I never seen such a strong guy.'

....

7 'He's jes' like a kid, ain't he.'

....

9 'He subsided, grumbling to himself, threatening the future cats which might dare to disturb the future rabbits.'

....

8 'This punk sure had it comin' to him. But – Jesus! He ain't hardly got no han' left.'

....

Check your answers on p. 70.

PAGES 66–82 – Death on the farm

1 Crooks teases Lennie and is frightened by his response.

2 Curley's wife reveals how lonely and how dangerous she is.

3 Lennie accidentally kills the puppy.

DID YOU KNOW?

Steinbeck was so fed up with people pestering him that he equipped a station wagon as a mobile study so that he could 'get away from it all' to write.

EXAMINER'S SECRET

The characters in a novel can use slang and bad language – but the student can't!

Lennie is left behind when George goes into town with the other ranch hands. He walks into Crooks's room. Crooks is a bitter, cynical person. It is often asked how much of this bitterness comes from his being a black man. Steinbeck rams home to the reader how few rights black people had when he reveals that Crooks could be lynched, without a trial, if Curley's wife so much as accuses him of trying to rape her. Lennie disarms Crooks's initial hostility with his simplicity. He reveals the plan to buy a farm, but the cynical Crooks teases Lennie about what will happen if George does not come back from town. Crooks is frightened by Lennie's response and reveals how lonely he is as a crippled black man on a farm of white men. The section with Crooks, Candy and Lennie in Crooks's room is almost a rest period before the final climax. Many authors step down the tension a little before a major climax, almost as if to rest the reader before a very demanding section.

Candy enters the room, this being the first time he has done so in all his years on the ranch. He talks about the farm he is going to move to with George and Lennie. Crooks pours scorn on the idea, as he has seen hundreds of men with a similar dream, but seems to be being won round when he realises how much of the money is actually there in the bank. He asks if he can come to work on the farm when it is bought, but he is interrupted by the appearance of Curley's wife. Candy tries to stand up to her with his new-found confidence in owning a part of his own small farm, but she crushes him. She also crushes Crooks, threatening him with a rape charge, a crime for which he would be hung without trial. Crooks withdraws his request to join the farm, his treatment from Curley's wife acting as a forcible reminder of the truths of his life.

TEST YOURSELF (PAGES 66–82)

WHO SAYS ...?

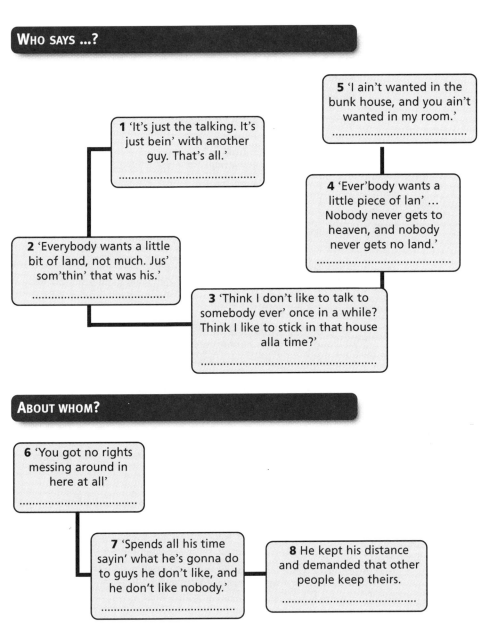

5 'I ain't wanted in the bunk house, and you ain't wanted in my room.'
....

1 'It's just the talking. It's just bein' with another guy. That's all.'
....

4 'Ever'body wants a little piece of lan' ... Nobody never gets to heaven, and nobody never gets no land.'
....

2 'Everybody wants a little bit of land, not much. Jus' som'thin' that was his.'
....

3 'Think I don't like to talk to somebody ever' once in a while? Think I like to stick in that house alla time?'
....

ABOUT WHOM?

6 'You got no rights messing around in here at all'
....

7 'Spends all his time sayin' what he's gonna do to guys he don't like, and he don't like nobody.'
....

8 He kept his distance and demanded that other people keep theirs.
....

Check your answers on p. 70.

PAGES 83–97 – Murder by mistake

❶ Curley's wife tells Lennie about herself and her life.

❷ Lennie panics and breaks her neck by accident.

❸ A man hunt starts out for Lennie, who has fled.

CHECKPOINT 12

Are we meant to like and/or sympathise with Curley's wife?

Lennie is in the barn stroking his puppy, which he has killed by accident. Curley's wife, bored and restless, enters and insists on sitting beside him. Lennie tries to stop her, remembering George's advice to have nothing to do with her, but she insists and talks about her life. Curley's wife reveals her loneliness. She is convinced that she could have joined a travelling show as a fifteen-year-old and become an actress. Another man she met at a dance promised her a part in the pictures, but he never wrote as promised to her. Convinced that her mother stole the letter, she married Curley out of spite and to get away from home.

CHECK THE FILM

In the 1992 film is Curley's wife lonely and pathetic, or someone who enjoys the destruction she causes?

Some feminist critics consider that *Of Mice and Men* encourages old-fashioned stereotypical images of women. They argue that Steinbeck sees the use of prostitutes as a man's right, and that the only woman who appears in the novel is an empty-headed sex doll who brings destruction to men. Others argue that the men in the novel are also frequently imperfect, or that Steinbeck actually has a huge sympathy for Curley's wife: she is portrayed as a pathetic figure, with her own unrealisable dream, married to a man she hates and with nothing to do except stare that marriage in the face. In her own way, perhaps she is as much of a victim as Lennie.

In basing his novel largely round a group of men and what we might see nowadays as 'macho' values, Steinbeck is writing in a firmly American tradition – the leading novelist of which is perhaps Ernest Hemingway. His concentration on male figures in *Of Mice and Men* allows him to examine a theme more closely studied in *The Grapes of Wrath*: in the America of the 1930s men are in charge. Yet both novels show how little anyone, male or female, is actually in control of their lives.

Gentle giant?

Curley's wife gets Lennie to admit that he likes stroking soft things and makes him stroke her hair. He strokes too hard and she cries out, frightening Lennie and making him cling on to her. When she will not stop screaming Lennie shakes her and by accident breaks her neck. He creeps away to the hiding place agreed with George.

There are warnings peppered throughout the novel about what will happen at the end. We know what happens when Lennie strokes anything – he does not know and cannot control his own strength, and so he kills the things he strokes. The death of the puppy warns us what will happen if Lennie touches Curley's wife, and we already know what happened when he touched a girl's dress in Weed. Yet despite all this, Steinbeck still makes Lennie seem very innocent. He simply likes to touch soft things, like a child. Tragically for him, he has the mind of a child but the body of a very strong man.

Candy discovers the body and brings George, guessing the murderer must be Lennie. George and Candy realise that this is the end of their dream. George slips back to the bunkhouse, so as not to be implicated in the murder. Candy tells the others about the death of Curley's wife, and Curley and Slim guess it must be Lennie who has broken her neck. The result is that the pursuers adopt a shoot-to-kill policy, ensuring that Lennie will die whatever happens. Lennie is also assumed to have stolen the pistol. Curley's cruelty is revealed when he tells the others to 'Shoot for his guts', to double him up (p. 96). They all set off to find Lennie, armed with shotguns.

Now take a break!

CHECKPOINT 13

Note the way that throughout the text Lennie is associated with animals. Would it be better if he was associated more with children?

CHECKPOINT 14

Are the lines, 'As happens sometimes, a moment settled and hovered ... much, much more than a moment' (p. 91) too 'poetic', too rich, in comparison with the rather objective, detached style Steinbeck adopts elsewhere?

WHO SAYS ...?

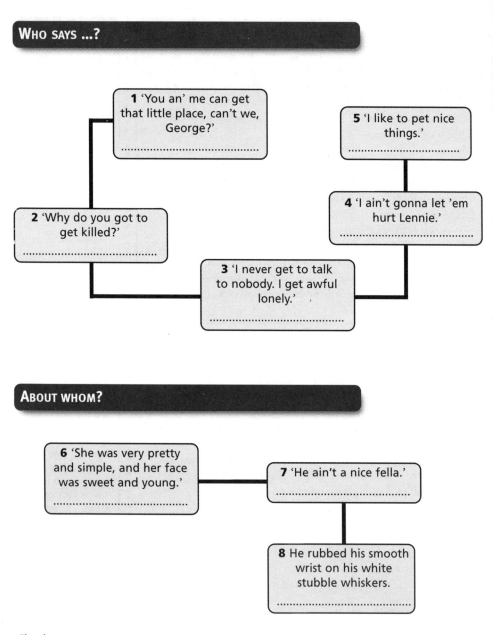

1 'You an' me can get that little place, can't we, George?'

....

5 'I like to pet nice things.'

....

4 'I ain't gonna let 'em hurt Lennie.'

....

2 'Why do you got to get killed?'

....

3 'I never get to talk to nobody. I get awful lonely.'

....

ABOUT WHOM?

6 'She was very pretty and simple, and her face was sweet and young.'

....

7 'He ain't a nice fella.'

....

8 He rubbed his smooth wrist on his white stubble whiskers.

....

Check your answers on p. 70.

PAGES 98–106

1 Lennie waits for George in the clearing by the pool.

2 He sees a vision of his Aunt Clara, which reprimands him.

3 A vision of a giant rabbit tells Lennie that George will leave him.

4 George comforts Lennie, then shoots him dead.

The section opens with a description reminiscent of the opening of the novel, particularly with its references to the heron and the water snake. Note the marvellous **image** of the sun blazing on the Gabilan Mountain, and the contrast with the shade of the pool.

EXAMINER'S SECRET

It is important to be very familiar with the climax of a novel, and understand how events have led up to it.

Lennie sits by the pool and drinks from it. He has a vision of his Aunt Clara, which reprimands him for letting George down. It is then replaced by a vision of a giant rabbit, which tells Lennie that George will leave him now, after what he has done. The visions are poetic and some critics have condemned them as being unrealistic and totally beyond the ability of a limited mind to generate. However, they provide a clear insight into Lennie's feelings at the close of the novel.

CHECKPOINT 15

Is it fair to say that the ending seems artificial, too obviously designed for effect rather than being true to life?

The mercy killing

Lennie is crying out for George when he appears. George talks quietly and apparently calmly to Lennie, and then 'woodenly' (p. 102) repeats the old story. As the climax approaches, Steinbeck includes fewer descriptive passages and adopts a shorter, more terse style, relying heavily on **dialogue**.

The sound of the hunters draws near. George tells Lennie to look away from him, across the river, to where he will almost be able to see the farm that they will buy. He shoots the unsuspecting Lennie in the back of the head with Carlson's Luger pistol. There is a tremendous **irony** in the fact that George takes Carlson's pistol in case he has to kill Lennie as an act of mercy. His decision to kill Lennie in order to protect him is based on the **paradox** of being cruel to be kind.

CHECKPOINT 16

Slim says of the murder, 'You hadda, George' (p. 106). Do you agree? What would have been the alternative?

Curley, Carlson, Slim and the others soon arrive, drawn by the shot. Only Slim understands what is going through George's mind, and reassures him that he has done the right thing: 'You hadda, George. I swear you hadda.' (p. 106). The two leave the others and go off down the highway for a drink.

TEST YOURSELF (PAGES 98–106)

WHO SAYS ...?

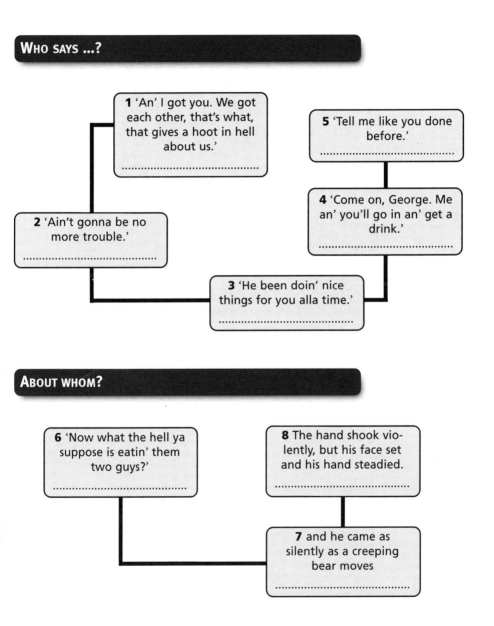

1 'An' I got you. We got each other, that's what, that gives a hoot in hell about us.'

....

2 'Ain't gonna be no more trouble.'

....

3 'He been doin' nice things for you alla time.'

....

5 'Tell me like you done before.'

....

4 'Come on, George. Me an' you'll go in an' get a drink.'

....

ABOUT WHOM?

6 'Now what the hell ya suppose is eatin' them two guys?'

....

8 The hand shook violently, but his face set and his hand steadied.

....

7 and he came as silently as a creeping bear moves

....

Check your answers on p. 70.

PART THREE

COMMENTARY

THEMES

FATE AND DESTINY

Sometimes a novel will hint at its **theme** through its title. The title of *Of Mice and Men* appears to be taken from the poem 'To a Mouse' by the Scottish poet Robert Burns (1759–96):

CHECK THE BOOK

Some readers consider *East of Eden* to be Steinbeck's greatest novel.

> The best laid schemes o' mice and men
> Gang aft agley
> And leave us nought but grief and pain
> For promised joy!

It is not difficult to see the link with Steinbeck's novel: 'Gang aft agley' means 'often go wrong'. George and Lennie's best-laid scheme for a small farm does go wrong, and leaves grief and pain where there should have been joy. Burns's poem also suggests that grief and pain, instead of joy, affect all creatures in nature, not just humanity. At the heart of the poem is the feeling that we are free to make our plans and lay our schemes, but far less free or likely to achieve them. Steinbeck never suggests that the likelihood of grief and pain should be a reason to stop humans laying their plans. We need to have these plans or dreams in order to survive, for all that they might hurt us.

DID YOU KNOW?

Steinbeck finally had a small, six-sided wooden hut built on a cliff top for him to write in.

The mention of mice by Burns also suggests something small and puny pitted against something overwhelmingly strong in the shape of Fate or Destiny. George and Lennie, and their dream, are similarly destined to be thwarted and shattered by inevitable forces over which they have no control.

This is perhaps the overriding theme of the novel – that humanity is small and fragile in comparison with the forces that control our lives, and that joy is something to be snatched while possible, but not something that most humans ever achieve for long.

There is no real thematic link between the mice in the title and the mice that Lennie likes to stroke. Lennie's mice are used rather as a motif that echoes his vulnerability throughout the novel.

DREAMS AND REALITY

One of Steinbeck's themes in *Of Mice and Men* is the dreams that people have. George and Lennie's dream is of a very small farm, a patch of land which they own themselves. It is a dream of working for themselves, of being independent, and it is a dream sufficiently powerful to draw in Candy and, temporarily, even the cynical Crooks. We know also it is a dream shared by many thousands of itinerant ranch hands.

Yet this is not the only dream in the novel. Curley's wife has a pathetic dream of being a movie star; and the ranch hands dream of being the cowboy heroes they read about in the pulp magazines.

THE AMERICAN DREAM

Some commentators have tied the dreams in the novel to a particular American Dream. For many years America welcomed the persecuted, the poor and the disadvantaged of the world, and it offered them the frontier. The line of civilisation steadily extended forward into virgin land until it reached the west coast. For those years the frontier was a line beyond which people were conditioned to believe that civilisation did not exist. Beyond it there was land for the taking, and a free and independent way of living where a man was answerable only to himself. People's old lives became history and new lives and new people could be created. Or so the story went. In truth the frontier was probably never like that, but the dream was necessary for people's survival and the belief that it might be true offered huge comfort to those who would never find out for themselves. By 1900 there was no more frontier, and many commentators believe that a new sense of pessimism crept into American culture. The hope of freedom, the hope of being an individual rather than a cog in a wheel, is certainly there in *Of Mice and Men*. So is the pessimism, because the dream is shattered, and shown to be unrealisable in the real world.

WWW. CHECK THE NET

A good resource for those wishing to do further research can be found at The Steinbeck Center: **www.steinbeck. org**

CHECKPOINT 17

Do you think that George's proposal to buy the nearby smallholding is a good idea?

It would be wrong to confine the dream only to American society. Steinbeck is using an American example to illustrate a general truth, the need people have to dream of a life that is better and which will combine freedom and personal fulfilment. The peasant farmer dreaming of the extra pig, the businessman dreaming of what the next promotion will bring, the young child fixing his eyes on the soccer or the rock star are all dreaming. Like George and Lennie, the dream will come true for only a very few, and those few are likely to find that achieving a dream rarely avoids stark reality.

PESSIMISM OR OPTIMISM?

CHECKPOINT 18

Identify the pessimistic and negative parts of the novel.

Is *Of Mice and Men* a pessimistic book? Its ending is unhappy, yet much in it is optimistic. George's care for Lennie, Lennie's adoration of George and the natural dignity of Slim are all positive, good things. Nor is Lennie's death wholly pessimistic. Lennie dies at the hand of the one man he trusts, painlessly, happy, free, in the open and still believing in his dream – as perhaps he might have died on the farm had they ever bought it. Lennie's death is an act of kindness, not of vengeance. To claim what happens as a good or a bad thing might be as senseless as to complain about the water snake that is killed by the heron at the end of the book. Both are parts of life and nature, so inevitable that human comment on them is almost superfluous.

A BALANCED BOOK

DID YOU KNOW?

The critic Mark Van Doren prophesied in 1937 that we would remember *Of Mice and Men* as long as we would remember a telephone call to the wrong number.

One of the key features of the book is balance, between the good and the bad, the happy and the unhappy. The dream is never realised, yet much good has been generated by the dreaming. Steinbeck never lectures us. He shows a vision of life that is neither black nor white. It has the simplicity of black, and the simplicity of white. He asks that you see life as it is, black and white side by side, rarely merging into grey.

PROTEST

Another frequently asked question is the extent to which *Of Mice and Men* is a political novel, or a novel of protest. The ranch hands get their fifty dollars a month and keep, seem to eat well and have a reasonable boss. To that extent the novel is not political. Nor does it concern itself with how the country is governed. If it protests, it does so against three social and political evils: racial discrimination, the treatment of old age and the plight of the farm worker who never reaps what he sows. Both Candy and Crooks are workers who will never see the benefits of their labour.

RACIAL PREJUDICE

Crooks illustrates racial prejudice. He is intelligent, reads books and, like any other human being, he needs warmth and companionship. He is denied these, not through any fault of his own but because he is black. Yet if there is a **theme** of racial prejudice here it is almost a sub-division of a wider theme, that of loneliness.

AGEISM

Candy is older than Crooks, and is a man who has outlived his usefulness. He is waiting to be cast on the scrapheap with no more ceremony than a worn-out domestic machine. Here again the larger and wider theme is one of loneliness, emphasised by Candy's relationship with his dog and his feelings when the dog is shot.

LONELINESS

Loneliness is a major **theme** in *Of Mice and Men*. George and Lennie stave it off by their relationship. It embitters Candy and Crooks. It kills Curley's wife. Steinbeck sees loneliness as a part of the human condition, something we are born with and something we either fight or succumb to all our lives:

> "Guys like us, that work on ranches, are the loneliest guys in the world" … Lennie broke in. "*But not us! An' why? Because … because I got you to look after me, and you got me to look after you, and that's why.*" (pp. 15–16)

As with many of the statements in the novel, Steinbeck offers no answers to loneliness, merely a graphic and moving portrayal of the problem. It confirms the impression of him as a writer who observes and brings things to life through the printed word. He is not someone writing with a grand game plan for how to change things. Indeed, some of the sadness and emotional power of the novel comes from our realisation that things cannot and will not change.

EXAMINER'S SECRET

An examiner can usually spot it if you simply write out what a critic has said. Always put ideas in your own words.

CHECK THE FILM

The 1939 version was ahead of its time in having the action start before the credits – almost unheard of at the time!

MYTH AND NOBILITY

Arthurian legend

CHECK THE FILM
Two modern versions are the Disney film *The Sword in the Stone*, based on the book by T.H. White, and the film *Excalibur*.

Steinbeck was fascinated by the 'Arthurian legend', essentially the story of England's King Arthur and his Knights of the Round Table. A real Arthur seems to have existed in the sixth century, but bore no relationship to the romantic figure of the later Middle Ages. The story that was created then, most notably by Sir Thomas Malory (d. 1471) in *Le Morte D'Arthur*, has exerted huge influence ever since. Arthur's story has become a **myth** – a story which seems to encapsulate a number of issues crucial to the experience of humanity, so crucial that the story is guaranteed to be recycled and recycled as each new generation arrives. Such myths have great power. That power is often attractive to an author. By their very survival myths have great strength and power over an audience or readership, and so by basing a story round a myth an author can tap into some of that myth's strength and appeal.

The power of myths

All of this might seem a long way off from George and Lennie. After all, there are few knights in armour or round tables in the book, and the characters are essentially lower class, not the nobility of the Arthurian legend. Yet the Arthurian legend has the Knight and the Squire team at its heart, leadership and service, which is the relationship between George and Lennie. The legend is also based on two pivotal points – the search or 'quest' for the Holy Grail (the cup that Christ drank from at the last supper before his crucifixion), and the betrayal of Arthur by his wife (Guinevere) and best friend (Sir Lancelot). George and Lennie's search for their piece of land is a quest for something that will bring peace to them, their farm bearing some comparison to the Holy Grail. There is also betrayal in *Of Mice and Men* and the death of a dream, a dream symbolised in the Arthurian legend by the Round Table.

DID YOU KNOW?
Steinbeck once said, 'Ideas are like rabbits. You get a couple and learn how to handle them, and pretty soon you have a dozen.'

The search for the Holy Grail – an unattainable dream

One reason for such a link is that it suggests the nobility of the working man, a common **theme** in Steinbeck's work. It is also a feature in some American writing that it sought to link itself to the older traditions of European writing, as if new writers in a new country felt somehow validated by their link with an older tradition as well as refreshed by being able to break from it. There is also an interesting area to examine in the tendency to **mythologise** aspects of American history, as in the Wild West and in the American Dream. All these point to a possible link with the Arthurian legend, but it is probably best not carried too far. Searching for a better future and betrayal are universal human experiences, and are found in many places and stories as well as in the Arthurian legend.

Mythologising American history: the working man

It is a little difficult to decide if the working man is merely a subject in the novel, or a theme in its own right. The characters in the book are drawn from a narrow social range, most being working men. Steinbeck reveals the immense diversity of personality and character to be found on a single ranch – the quick-wittedness and loyalty of George, the slowness of Lennie, the natural dignity and leadership of Slim, the bitter, ingrowing cynicism of Crooks, the brutality of Carlson, the superficiality of Whit and the sad fatalism of Candy.

BRAIN VERSUS BRAWN?

There is a tendency in Steinbeck's novels to rate the person with practical skills above the person with intellectual ability. This might appear strange from a highly intelligent writer, but it is a sub-theme in American culture, again derived from the **myth** or dream of the frontier. The frontier man had to build his own house, farm his own crops, deliver his own animals of their young, mend and make agricultural machinery, make his own cartridges, skin and cure animal hide and brew his own drink – at least in legend! Yet with all these practical skills (in effect the ability to do at least part of the job of the modern builder, farmer, veterinary surgeon, agricultural engineer, gunsmith, tanner, brewer and carpenter) frontier man often had only one book, a copy of the Holy Bible.

Of Mice and Men does not condemn intellectuals. It merely ignores them and sees real life as taking place outside of their boundaries.

Does Steinbeck attempt to arouse your pity by a false, unreal concentration on misfits? If so, the balance is at least partially put

DID YOU KNOW?

Steinbeck was described by his last wife as a 'Mr Fixit' who loved to make things in wood and metal.

CHECKPOINT 19

The pairing of a smaller man with a larger man, or a clever man with a stupid man, is typical of comedy. Can you think of examples?

right by the portrayal of Slim, by which Steinbeck seems to be saying that natural leaders and people of authority will emerge in every walk of life.

STRUCTURE

Of Mice and Men is a short novel. Sometimes these are described as novellas. The book has no chapter divisions, but falls into six readily identifiable sections, all except the first and last of which are set in the bunk-house.

A PLAY-LIKE STRUCTURE

The division of the novel into six clear sections bears comparison with the separate scenes of a play, because:

- Each 'scene' has a clearly identified setting.
- The setting is simple and often very visual.
- The plot progresses chronologically, i.e. in the order in which it actually happens.
- There is a lot of dialogue and speech.
- The characters and the setting are often very visual.

There is therefore a dramatic element to the structure of the novel as well as to its style.

Why are there no chapter divisions? Probably because in such a short novel Steinbeck does not want to break up the flow of the text. Chapter divisions might also reduce the feeling of inevitability in the novel.

INEVITABILITY: CLUMSY OR DELIBERATE?

Steinbeck has been criticised for making the ending seem inevitable, and for dropping too many clumsy hints as to what will happen. The hints are:

- Lennie's killing of mice

DID YOU KNOW?

Steinbeck himself dramatised *Of Mice and Men* for the stage.

- What happened between Lennie and the girl in Weed
- The killing of Candy's dog
- The fight with Curley
- The killing of the puppy
- The emphasis on Lennie's vast strength
- The girl's interest in Lennie
- George's oft-repeated assertions that the girl will bring nothing but trouble .

The defence against this charge is that Steinbeck is not writing a novel of suspense, but a novel about characters. However, it might still be felt that some of the hints he offers are rather heavy-handed. Remember that many types of literature do not require you to be kept in suspense.

SIMPLICITY

Of Mice and Men follows a simple chronological, or real time, structure. There are no flashbacks to previous episodes and there is no rushing forward to see snippets of the future, both common techniques in many modern novels. The story commences on a Thursday evening and its climax is reached on the following Sunday afternoon. The keynote of the plot and structure in this novel is simplicity.

CHARACTERS

GEORGE

George Milton and Slim are the heroes of *Of Mice and Men*. George is, in Slim's words, 'a smart little guy' (p. 40). It is typical of George – he is very modest – that he denies this claim, pointing out that if he was really smart, he would be farming for himself and not doing all the work for other people. One of the points made in the novel as a whole is that intelligence on its own is worth little. If it were worth much, then both George and Crooks would be rich men, because both are obviously intelligent.

DID YOU KNOW?

The *New York Times* described the novel as 'a thriller, a gripping tale ... that you will not set down until it is finished'.

Small
Intelligent
Practical
Caring
Modest

 CHECK THE FILM
Sinise, who plays George in the 1992 version is a real Steinbeck fan. As a young man his favourite book was *Of Mice and Men*, and he has also starred in a stage production of *The Grapes of Wrath*. Sinise directed the 1992 film too!

Economic reasons make it hard for George to possess his own small farm. There are other difficulties as well, the main one being Lennie. If George is to look after Lennie, probably the only way he can do it is to move from ranch to ranch. The longer the pair stay in one place, the more likely it is that Lennie will get himself into trouble. Permanent employment is not therefore an option, unless George ditches Lennie.

So why does George stay with Lennie? George frequently tells Lennie how much freedom he, George, would enjoy if he was not with Lennie: 'God a'mighty, if I was alone I could live so easy.' (p. 12). He says it so often that Lennie knows the speech off by heart, just as he does the speech about the dream of a farm.

Undoubtedly George has come to like Lennie, and he feels a sense of duty and responsibility towards him. But there is more to their partnership than this. George is a thinker. All around him he sees the rootless, nomadic farm workers, many of them lonely, ineffectual and lost. The companionship with Lennie staves off loneliness, but it also gives George a role in life, a clear task, looking after Lennie. Early on it made George feel superior. Now it simply makes him different, and even gives him status. In addition, just as there is trouble in being with Lennie, so there is strength, huge strength; as George says to Slim: 'We kinda look after each other' (p. 36). Who would fight George if they knew they would have to fight Lennie as well?

George is a good judge of other people's characters. He can sense that Curley and his wife will bring trouble, and that Slim is a good man. He is quiet, causing no trouble in the bunk-house, modest and clearly a good worker. He is clean-living, partly because he needs to save his money if ever he is to buy his farm and cannot waste money in the brothel or in the pool room, but also because of his temperament. He is appalled by Lennie drinking 'scummy' water (p. 5), appalled by the prospect of the previous occupant of his bunk having left lice in the bedding. He is a peaceful man but fights when he has to. One senses a certain delight when he tells Lennie to 'get' Curley (p. 63).

Some critics have argued that George shows a great capacity for 'moral growth' over the course of the novel. They argue that his relationship with Lennie matures him, forces him to think more and increases his awareness of moral problems. He certainly has grown up in the past as a result of his relationship with Lennie. Early on he used to show off the power he had over Lennie – 'Made me seem God damn smart alongside of him' (p. 41), forcing him to do stupid and, in one instance, life-threatening things. His sense of shame soon stopped him. However, his shooting of Lennie adds nothing new to what we know of him. It is merely the result of everything we have learnt about him and, like so much else in the novel, is almost inevitable. Features which George has possessed all along combine to force him to shoot Lennie.

George is a moral person, as shown by his distaste for brothels and his disgust at Curley telling the story about a glove full of Vaseline. It is George's morality that tells him Lennie cannot be allowed to run away, because this time he has actually killed someone.

George is full of compassion and it is this which makes him wish for a clean death for Lennie, rather than a lynching or a lifetime spent cooped up in jail.

George is a responsible person. He brought Lennie to the farm, and so the responsibility for what happened and the responsibility for the punishment are his. He accepts them, with great heroism. Slim spots that George had to do what he does to Lennie: 'You hadda, George. I swear you hadda.' (p. 106). No one else in the novel is shown as understanding.

George has made sacrifices in order to look after Lennie. When he kills him he makes the greatest sacrifice of all. Lennie dies with the words and expression of their shared dream on his lips and face. When he dies, so does the dream, killed by the man who brought it into being.

The tragedy of George is that his best features have led him to kill the thing and the person he loves most. There is no practical reason why George should not still buy the farm with Candy. Emotionally it is another story. The dream is dead with Lennie and because of Lennie.

CHECK THE FILM

A 1981 version for television was made as the result of a lifelong ambition on the part of producer/star Robert Blake. It is hard to get hold of, but is seen as an above average production.

Simple
Childlike
Physically strong
Innocent

 DID YOU KNOW?
Steinbeck based Lennie on a real person he had known, who was sent to a lunatic asylum for stabbing a ranch boss in the stomach with a pitchfork.

LENNIE

Lennie Small is a child's mind in a man's body, as Slim observes: 'He's jes' like a kid' (p. 44). But, as George replies, while Lennie's mind is extremely childlike, 'he's so strong' (p. 44). He is a half wit, a simpleton, and his tragedy is that his mind has never learnt how to control his body. He is amazed and upset when his mice and his puppy die, unable to realise that it is not their fragility but his strength that are to blame.

Lennie is also, as is pointed out, 'a nice fella' (p. 36). After his strength his most obvious feature is his innocence, an innocence so transparent and obvious that you cannot help but sympathise with him, and feel some of the same affection that George so obviously feels for him. Steinbeck often describes him in terms of an animal, perhaps pointing to his being a creature of instinct rather than a being of rational or intellectual thought, but this does nothing to lessen his humanity. Lennie is like an animal in that his mind and his body cannot cope with the complexities of human life. Steinbeck compares Lennie to an animal too: when we first meet him he drags his feet 'the way a bear drags his paws' and drinks from the pool 'like a horse' (p. 4). The only way he can cope is to be a like a tame dog, tethered always to his master George and never let out of his master's sight.

Yet Lennie is not totally straightforward. He has an animal cunning that he can bring into play. For instance, at the start of the novel, he realises that George will feel guilty about losing his temper after he has taken away Lennie's mouse. Lennie plays on George's feelings of guilt that he has robbed a child of a prized possession. As a result of this Lennie gets the sympathy that he wants from George. Lennie is cunning and aware in another sense. His instinct tells him that the ranch is 'no good place' to be (p. 34), and events prove him correct.

Some critics have felt that Lennie's tendency to hold on when he panics is unrealistic, but anyone who has life-saved and tried to break the grip of someone they think is drowning will know that hanging on is a trait shared by all human beings, and not just those who are mentally retarded.

A more serious criticism is directed against the two visions Lennie has at the end of the novel, one of Aunt Clara and one of a gigantic rabbit, both of whom reprimand Lennie. Some would argue that Lennie has been portrayed as someone whose intellect makes it difficult for him to speak at all, never mind give a voice to two other people and construct a **dialogue**. The effect of these two 'visions' could therefore be seen as false and artificial, an artistic intervention in a novel which has above all been realistic. On the other hand, it could be argued that both Aunt Clara and the rabbit feature largely in Lennie's memory and his mind, they come 'from out of Lennie's head' (p. 99): in one he is remembering what was said to him and in the other merely putting George's words into the mouth of a much-loved animal.

Lennie is both a victim and a **symbol**. It is not his fault that he was born without the full mental faculties of others, and he becomes a victim of a world that chooses not to understand or make allowances for him. He is also a symbol of a world that is rarely just or fair and that exercises a cruel judgement on those who live within it. Only one of those who suffer in *Of Mice and Men* is blameworthy for what he does and deserves his punishment, and that is Curley. The remainder – Candy, Crooks, Curley's wife, George and above all Lennie – suffer despite their basic innocence.

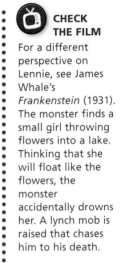

CHECK THE FILM
For a different perspective on Lennie, see James Whale's *Frankenstein* (1931). The monster finds a small girl throwing flowers into a lake. Thinking that she will float like the flowers, the monster accidentally drowns her. A lynch mob is raised that chases him to his death.

SLIM

Slim receives the longest introductory description of any character in the novel (pp. 34–5). Those who wish to sum up Slim need look no further than this description, which says everything there is to say about him. The remainder of the novel simply reinforces the points made in this introduction and adds nothing new. The length of this introduction shows how deeply interested Steinbeck was in Slim. The description given of him, containing the words 'majesty', 'gravity' 'authority' and 'understanding beyond thought', could be used without disrespect of an elder statesman, a great teacher or a philosopher. It might seem ludicrous that it is applied to a ranch hand, albeit a very skilled one.

It also begs the question as to why someone so gifted is forced to live in a bunk-house, eating another person's food and condemned to live

Honest

Dignified

Gifted

Conscience of novel

Aristocratic

with anyone the boss appoints to work on the ranch. Slim is the product of Steinbeck's desire to show that nobility of mind and purpose can be found in all sections of society. It is also a part of his mission to raise the status of migrant workers, something he brought to near perfection in his later novel *The Grapes of Wrath* (1939).

It is Slim who understands why George and Lennie work the ranches as a pair, and he understands the bond between them. It is Slim who comes to the only correct judgement of Lennie: 'Guy don't need no sense to be a nice fella' (p. 41). It is Slim who is the only person who understands why George has to kill Lennie, and it is Slim who is the only person who comes near to understanding what the personal cost to George has been of doing what he has done. To that extent Slim is the conscience of the novel, the voice of truth and its anchor point.

 DID YOU KNOW?

In his acceptance speech for the Nobel Prize in 1962, Steinbeck said that a writer should expose human 'faults and failures'; but that any worthy author will 'passionately believe in the perfectibility of man'.

Does Steinbeck give too much respect to those with practical skills, and ignore those with intellectual ability? Perhaps the answer depends rather too much on which set of skills one was born with. Slim makes a point that few critics of the novel have spotted. Like George, Slim is intelligent, that intelligence being shown in a capacity to sum up situations instantly rather than in any ability to pass examinations. Slim is someone whose self-respect derives from the fact that he does what he is paid to do superbly. In his case it is driving mules or other animals. In another person's case it could be playing superb soccer, writing the best book ever on Shakespeare or cooking the best meals in town. The nature of the skill is not what matters; it is mastery of that skill which counts. Those who know what they can do and are allowed by life to do it well are, in Steinbeck's eyes, the true aristocracy of our world. Slim is just such an aristocrat and in his portrayal Steinbeck is telling us that we should not be surprised to find an aristocrat living in the bunk-house of a Californian ranch. This aristocracy earns its spurs by what it is and what it does, not where it was born or to whom.

CANDY

Candy has lost his right hand in a farm accident and is now reduced to the meanest job on the ranch, that of 'swamper' or menial cleaner: 'I ain't much good with on'y one hand' (p. 59). His function in the novel is to show you what happens to an old man beset by physical disability, loneliness and rejection.

One-handed
Pathetic
Subservient
Stooped
Devoted to his dog

Candy is a pathetic figure. He has lost all control over his life and can only pass his time through being subservient to others, yet getting his own back on them through gossip. Only on two occasions in the novel does he stand up to people: once when he joins in on the attack on Curley, and again when he tells Curley's wife what he thinks of her. In each case his defiance is short-lived, and its early end serves only to make him appear even more pathetic. In that defiance we see both what Candy might have been and what he has become.

Against all this is the fact that you are shown just how little it would take to revitalise Candy – ten acres and a few animals. We see Candy (along with Lennie) 'grinning with delight' (p. 61) when he plans the ranch with George and Lennie. You are being asked to think how many other outwardly worthless people need so little to make them figures of respect.

Candy provides a parallel to George and Lennie in that he relies on his dog – 'I'm so used to 'im' (p. 46) – just as George and Lennie are an elevated version of a master–dog relationship. Candy clings to his dog, despite all that logic and common sense dictate. In much the same manner, George and Lennie cling to each other, also perhaps despite the dictates of common sense.

The dog's death reveals that Candy is a human being with all human feelings and emotions, and as such should not be lightly dismissed. Candy, rather like his dog, is old, infirm and weak. One of the strongest statements in *Of Mice and Men* is that such people are worthy of our attention and our respect.

CROOKS

Like Candy, Crooks is an example of Steinbeck's compassion and a further illustration of the way in which loneliness (see **Themes**) can corrupt and destroy a man. His cynicism about the world is summed up when he says, 'Nobody gets to heaven, and nobody gets no land' (p. 73). Crooks has a double burden. He is not only a black man in a society that immediately relegates non-whites to a sub-human status, but also partly disabled in a society that values human beings simply on their ability to provide a service.

'Stable buck'
Crippled
Pained
Proud

The true horror of Crooks's situation is revealed when he dares to challenge a white woman married to a white man. Curley's wife has done little to warrant respect, though she may have your sympathy. This girl, by virtue of her race rather than her attributes as a human being, can crush Crooks in little more than a sentence: 'You know what I can do to you if you open your trap?' (p. 80). As a white woman, even the accusation of rape against a black man will result in a lynching. It is unjust, unfair and against all concepts of natural justice – yet it is the way of the world of this novel.

But if Steinbeck is compassionate, he is also fair. Crooks is not treated badly by the other ranch hands and is described as a 'Nice fella' (p. 20) by Candy. He is also given a room of his own, albeit a room in which he also works and which has a manure heap just outside the window. Crooks himself feels that he is unwanted ''Cause I'm black' (p. 68).

Crooks's structural role in the novel is to appear two thirds of the way through and forewarn and prepare you for the imminent destruction of George and Lennie's dream.

In creating a **character** such as Crooks, Steinbeck is following a time-hallowed tradition. First, find a character in whom you have to believe, because he or she is so convincingly drawn and you identify with them. Then expose him or her to a potent dream and show him or her warming to it as you have warmed to it. Finally, show the character realising that the dream is nothing more than a dream, a fantasy doomed to failure because the real world does not allow dreams to come to fruition. Like Crooks, we want to believe in the dream despite everything we know. And like Crooks, we come to realise that it is an impossible dream.

CURLEY

Curley is a spoilt, restless young man with a grudge against the world. A small man, he is incapable of meeting someone bigger without taking a dislike to them: as the swamper says, 'He's alla time picking scraps with big guys.' (p. 28). Curley seems set on proving to the world that he is a big man in all but size. He has had some success as an amateur boxer and boxing has become an obsession with him, so much so that every person he meets is seen as a possible opponent.

Curley makes obscene allusions to his young wife and goes to the brothel on Saturday nights. He then complains when his wife appears to want to take her pleasure in a similar vein. He is a laughing stock with the other men for his obsession that she is behaving herself – Whit says that 'Curley's pants is just crawlin' with ants' (p. 52) – and he is hated by his new wife.

Small
Unpleasant
Jealous
Unfaithful
Cruel

Curley is not unintelligent, and has a form of cunning. He is also cruel and insensitive, capable only of seeing the world through his own eyes and as a result possessed of a supreme selfishness. He is a man bordering on evil, and is by far the most unpleasant and unattractive character in the novel. His inability to control his wife or even vaguely to understand her brings about the final tragedy of Lennie's death. He is to blame, just as much as his wife and as Lennie. His tragedy is that he will never accept that blame. For Curley, it is always someone else's fault.

CURLEY'S WIFE

Curley's wife is a 'tart' (p. 29) and may well be 'jail bait' (p. 33) in the eyes of the ranch hands, but she is never really evil. Her punishment outweighs any crimes she may have committed. Perhaps she could even have been a loving wife had she met the right man. As Steinbeck explains in a letter, she would have been a slave to any man who 'treated her like a person'.

Flirtatious
Lonely
Misunderstood
Dreamer

We know more about Steinbeck's feelings towards Curley's wife than

about any other character. In the famous 'Miss Luce' letter, he wrote to the actress playing the part in the stage version of the novel, saying how he saw the character. In the letter Steinbeck says she is essentially a good and trusting person who grew up 'in an atmosphere of fighting and suspicion'. Her pretence of hardness is largely a sham. It is all she knows. She is not particularly over-sexed, but has been forced to recognise that her sexuality is the only weapon she has, and the only thing that gets her noticed. She was almost certainly a virgin before she married Curley because she has had it preached at her so hard that it is the only way she can get a husband. In Steinbeck's words to the actress, 'She had only that one thing to sell and she knew it'. A comparison has been made here (though not by Steinbeck) with another semi-mythical figure in American entertainment, the film actress Marilyn Monroe, capable of exuding a huge sexuality but combining it with innocence, vulnerability and an inability to enjoy sex.

**CHECK
THE FILM**

Curley's wife is played by Sherilyn Fenn in the 1992 film version. True to the novel, she is not named.

There is, of course, a danger in knowing so much about what the author intended the character to be like. If every author's intention was what actually got written then every novel would be a bestseller. An author can tell us how he intended the character to be; the reader is the one who decides what is actually described. Is there a case for seeing Curley's wife as rather more of a hard case than Steinbeck intended her to be?

THE BOSS

A stocky, short little man. He is a reasonable sort of person, who gets angry at times but buys whisky for the hands at Christmas. He is a very distant figure. His wife is never mentioned and it might be assumed that she is dead.

CARLSON

'A powerful, big-stomached man' (p. 36), an insensitive ranch hand. He objects to the smell of Candy's dog, pressurises Candy to have it shot and does the business himself with evident satisfaction, using his own Luger pistol. This is the same pistol that George later uses to shoot Lennie.

WHIT

A young ranch hand, who finds a letter in a magazine written by an ex-worker at the ranch. He is very superficial, and has no real involvement in the plot of the novel or its **themes**, except as the hand who is sent into the town to fetch the deputy sheriff after the murder of Curley's wife.

LANGUAGE AND STYLE

There are almost two separate styles in *Of Mice and Men*. One is descriptive and almost poetic in its intensity, the other down-to-earth and colloquial. Steinbeck manages to blend these two styles together with almost complete fluency. This blending is one of the reasons why *Of Mice and Men* is such a remarkable novel.

DESCRIPTIVE STYLE

This owes its success to Steinbeck's eye for minute observation of nature and his gift for unusual **metaphors** and **similes**. As one example, he describes the head of a water-snake as being 'like a periscope' (p. 9). At first reading this simile might seem totally out of place. A periscope is a man-made object of steel and glass, part of a machine designed for war and found at sea rather than in the confines of a small pool in a river. Yet the **image** does work:

EXAMINER'S SECRET
The examiner will be impressed if you can identify metaphors and talk about the effects they have. Keep a list as you read *Of Mice and Men*.

- It is startling and unexpected, and so focuses your attention on what is being described.

- Visually the water snake and the periscope are similar, with both being upright and ploughing through the water.

- The snake's eyes are in its head, just as the periscope provides eyes for the submarine.

- A submarine is a machine of death, but so perhaps is the snake, hunting for its kill in the shadows.

Steinbeck's descriptive style can also be very powerful when he uses straight descriptive language. For example, George has to stop Lennie from drinking from a pool at the start of the novel. The water is 'scummy' (p. 5). This is a simple, factual description of the water.

As well as describing the water, the description manages to tell us how very little common sense Lennie has. Also, by hinting at dirt and corruption, it might even prepare us for a dark ending to the novel.

Steinbeck's style is also very economical. He never pours hundreds of descriptive words into a paragraph, but describes a few bare essentials to give a flavour of the scene.

Use of light

Steinbeck loves to use light in his descriptive passages. The light flaming on the Gabilan Mountains is a recurrent image. Steinbeck is fascinated by sunlight. He describes a bar of it shining into the bunk-house:

CHECK THE BOOK

Steinbeck's *The Grapes of Wrath* has a very similar style to *Of Mice and Men*.

> … the sun threw a bright dust-laden bar through one of the side windows, and in and out of the beam flies shot like rushing stars.
>
> (p. 19)

Later Curley's wife enters the bunk-house and 'the rectangle of sunshine in the doorway was cut off' (p. 32) – the light being used as a **symbol** for the way that her stupidity is going to cut short her own life and Lennie's, and destroy George and Lennie's dream.

Sound and vision

Steinbeck also uses sound in his descriptions, particularly the background sounds that add so much to our imagination of the colour and vision of a scene. One example is 'the thuds and occasional clangs of a horseshoe game' in the yard (p. 39); another the sounds heard by George as he prepares to kill Lennie:

> … the leaves rustled … And the shouts of men sounded again, this time much closer than before.
>
> (p. 103)

As the men get nearer, the shouts grow louder and the sense of tension is increased. The accuracy of Steinbeck's observation helps you to believe that you are an eyewitness to the events described.

THE LANGUAGE OF DIALOGUE

Steinbeck makes heavy use of **dialogue**, and recreates directly the vernacular, slangy and colloquial language of the ranch hands. He writes as they speak, and recreates their language with unfaltering accuracy. In doing so he uses swear words and contortions of grammar that would have an English teacher in hospital (my favourite is 'Ain't got no relatives nor nothing' [p. 60], which in grammatical terms is actually a treble negative, something almost impossible to achieve). The language may be grammatically incorrect, yet it is vivid, alive and full of colour. Steinbeck also uses it for comic effect. Slim is described as the aristocrat of the ranch, its true king. After this introduction, his first words are, 'It's brighter'n a bitch outside' (p. 35), a line which no king would use and which brings you back down to earth very rapidly. Though Steinbeck's characters use slang, when they are not speaking Steinbeck writes using relatively simple vocabulary, words that require little or no explanation. He never shows off in his writing, using learned or obscure words to impress the reader with his cleverness.

Writing dialogue and trying to recreate the voice of 'ordinary' people is surprisingly difficult. Firstly, the more the writer tries to recreate the actual sound of people talking, the more difficult to read the language can be on the page. Throughout *Of Mice and Men* Steinbeck leaves the ends off words to show how George and the others speak: '… an' I'd get a job an' make up the res', an' you could sell eggs an' stuff like that' (p. 60). Yet the language always remains understandable, as well as allowing us to 'hear' the sound of it in our head.

There is **irony** in much of Steinbeck's dialogue. Candy suggests Crooks's room is cosy and that he is lucky to have a room on his own. Crooks replies that it's 'swell' (p. 74), particularly with a manure pile under the window.

It is worth noting that Steinbeck never speaks to the reader directly. Some authors lecture the reader directly. Steinbeck either lets his characters speak, or describes the background they exist in. There is no moralising from the author in *Of Mice and Men*, no lecturing the reader and no sermons.

DID YOU KNOW?
The two key aspects of Steinbeck's writing – his use of colloquial language and his descriptive style – have been described as 'jewelled metaphors' and the 'practical language of fact'

EXAMINER'S SECRET
Never start an essay unless you know what your conclusion is and how you want to finish it.

RESOURCES

HOW TO USE QUOTATIONS

One of the secrets of success in writing essays is the way you use quotations. There are five basic principles:

1 Put inverted commas at the beginning and end of the quotation.

2 Write the quotation exactly as it appears in the original.

3 Do not use a quotation that repeats what you have just written.

4 Use the quotation so that it fits into your sentence.

5 Keep the quotation as short as possible.

Quotations should be used to develop the line of thought in your essays. Your comment should not duplicate what is in your quotation. For example:

> Those who work on the ranch seem to think that the boss is a reasonable employer. George asks what he is like, and Candy's response is this, '"He's a nice fella," the swamper agreed. "You got to take him right"' (p. 26).

Far more effective is to write:

> Those who work on the ranch seem to agree with Candy that the boss is 'a nice fella'.

However, the most sophisticated way of using the writer's words is to embed them into your sentence:

> You know that George has done the right thing when Slim says, 'You hadda, George. I swear you hadda' (p. 106).

When you use quotations in this way, you are demonstrating the ability to use text as evidence to support your ideas – not simply including words from the original to prove you have read it.

SEWORK ESSAY

an hour or so at the start of your work to plan what you do.

ll the points you feel are needed to cover the task. Collect references of information and quotations that will support you have to say. A helpful tool is the highlighter pen: this painstaking copying and enables you to target precisely what want to use.

on what you consider to be the main points of the essay. sum up your argument in a single sentence, which could be ing sentence of your essay. Depending on the essay title, it e a statement about a character: Slim is the real hero of the ecause he is the only character who reaches the right ons about everything; an opinion about setting: The y with which Steinbeck describes the countryside around S nd the life of the ranch hand – both of which he had ly experienced – gives authority to everything else he sta the novel; or a judgement on a theme: I think loneliness is the theme in Of Mice and Men because more people suffer fron the novel than from anything else.

- Make short essay plan. Use the first paragraph to introduce the argument you wish to make. In the following paragraphs develop this argument with details, examples and other possible points of view. Sum up your argument in the last paragraph. Check you have answered the question.

- Write the essay, remembering all the time the central point you are making.

- On completion, go back over what you have written to eliminate careless errors and improve expression. Read it aloud to yourself, or, if you are feeling more confident, to relative or friend.

If you can, try to type you essay, using a word processor. This will allow you to correct and improve your writing without spoiling its appearance.

EXAMINER'S SECRET

It is good presentation to underline the title of the novel throughout an essay, or print it in italics if you are using a word-processor.

EXAMINER'S SECRET

Use clear, formal language, not slang or colloquial language.

SITTING THE EXAMINATION

EXAMINER'S SECRET
The most common thing that students get wrong is not to answer the question!

Examination papers are carefully designed to give you the opportunity to do your best. Follow these handy hints for exam success:

BEFORE YOU START

- Make sure you know the subject of the examination so that you are properly prepared and equipped.

- You need to be comfortable and free from distractions. Inform the invigilator if anything is off-putting, e.g. a shaky desk.

- Read the instructions, or rubric, on the front of the examination paper. You should know by now what you have to do but check to reassure yourself.

- Observe the time allocation – and follow it carefully. If they recommend 60 minutes for Question 1 and 30 minutes for Question 2, it is because Question 1 carries twice as many marks.

- Consider the mark allocation. You should write a longer response for 4 marks than for 2 marks.

WRITING YOUR RESPONSES

EXAMINER'S SECRET
Try and read round the novel. Evidence of extra reading will broaden your understanding of the text, and impress your examiner.

- Use the questions to structure your response, e.g. question: 'The endings of X's poems are always particularly significant. Explain their importance with reference to two poems.' The first part of your answer will describe the ending of the first poem; the second part will look at the ending of the second poem; the third part will be an explanation of the significance of the two endings.

- Write a brief draft outline of your response.

- A typical 30-minute examination essay is probably between 400 and 600 words in length.

- Keep your writing legible and easy to read, using paragraphs to show the structure of your answers.

- Spend a couple of minutes afterwards quickly checking for obvious errors.

W**HEN YOU HAVE FINISHED**

- Don't be downhearted – if you found the examination difficult, it is probably because you really worked at the questions. Let's face it, they are not meant to be easy!

- Don't pay too much attention to what your friends have to say about the paper. Everyone's experience is different and no two people ever give the same answers.

I**MPROVE YOUR GRADE**

W**HAT DOES THE EXAMINER WANT?**

There are certain very practical things the examiner is looking for. When your exam script or essay is marked the examiner looks at the **content**:

- Whether or not you have understood the issues in the work

- Whether or not you have answered the question

- Whether or not you have responded personally to what you have read

However, marks are also awarded for **expression** and **presentation,** including such things as:

- Line of argument: do you know what it is you want to say, and have you said it clearly?

- Paragraphing: have you split your answer up into clear paragraphs, does each paragraph have its own clear topic and are the links between the paragraphs clear?

- Quotations: have you quoted, accurately and appropriately, from the text to support the points you have made?

- Style: have you written in a suitable, formal style?

EXAMINER'S SECRET
The introduction and the conclusion of an essay are often the best places in which to refer to other books by the same author.

Answering the Question

The one thing that you must do is to answer the question. It is terribly tempting if you have read *Of Mice and Men* and feel it has a lot to say about racism to write that viewpoint down when the exam comes along, even if the examiner has not asked about it. Unfortunately, it does not matter how good your answer is. If it is not an answer to the question the examiner has asked then it will get no marks.

A good way of checking that you are answering the question is to write a *topic sentence* as the first sentence of each paragraph. All this means is that you sum up what you want to say in that paragraph in the first sentence, as in:

The treatment of Candy shows that racism is a major theme in *Of Mice and Men.*

Then look back to the essay title. If it is 'How prominent a theme is racism in *Of Mice and Men*?' then your paragraph will be fine. If the question is, 'How important are the minor characters in *Of Mice and Men*?', then your topic sentence shows that you are answering a different question, and you need to think again.

Style and Language

EXAMINER'S SECRET
Don't tell the examiner how easy or hard the question is ... you are there to answer the question, not comment upon it!

The most difficult questions to answer are often those on style and language. One of the most common questions in examinations is along the lines of 'Show how Steinbeck treats the theme of loneliness'. The examiner does not want you just to say *what* the author says, but *how* he says it—what we talk about as an author's style. Remember the important areas in discussing a novel: language; **characterisation**; plot; structure. Areas you can look at include:

- THE CHOICE OF WORDS: are they simple or complex? From ordinary language, or specialised?

- METHODS OF CHARACTERISATION: does the author let the character describe themselves by what they say, by what they do or by both? Does the author tell you what to think about characters and make judgements on them, or does he or she let you make up your own mind on the basis of what he shows you? Does the author characterise by linking a character with strong physical features, or even by giving him a name that is very descriptive?

- USE OF COMPARISONS: look at **simile** and **metaphor** in particular. Why does the author compare one thing or person with another? Is there a link between the similes and metaphors that s/he uses – are many of them based on animals, for example, or drawn from nature?

- PLOT STRUCTURE: is the plot told chronologically, in the order in which events took place, or does the author use flash-back techniques, or take you forward into the future? How do we learn about the plot – through the characters telling us the story, or through the author doing so? Does our impression of the plot change depending on which character tells us about it?

- BOOK DIVISIONS: how is the book divided up? Into chapter headings, or in some other way?

EXAMINER'S SECRET
Make your paragraphs link together so your argument is logically presented.

PLANNING

Time spent on thinking and planning before you begin an essay is *not* time wasted. You can afford to spend 5–10 minutes jotting down some notes and arranging them in some sort of order before you start to write an essay or an examination answer. The result will be better if you do!

WRITING

As you are writing the essay, develop an internal mechanism that makes you ask 'Am I answering the question?'

Avoid padding in your essay and unnecessary narrative. Never simply tell the story of the novel to the examiner – s/he can read it in the original if that is all s/he is interested in.

Remember essays are formal pieces of writing. Something like, **'Slim is dead cool, but Curley's wife is a cow and deserves to be wasted'** is fine if you are talking to a friend, but instant death if you use it in an essay or an examination. What you *meant* to say was:

EXAMINER'S SECRET
Develop one idea in each paragraph, and always have an idea to develop in a paragraph.

EXAMINER'S SECRET

Always remember to write legibly. If the examiner cannot read what you have written he or she cannot give you a mark for it.

Slim is an admirable figure and a hero in the novel, whilst Curley's wife is a silly and dangerous women who brings trouble to everything she touches.

Flattery

Resist the urge to flatter the writer or the novel. Comments such as, 'Steinbeck is an absolutely brilliant author and *Of Mice and Men* is one of the best books ever to have been written in the history of novels' show nothing about your understanding of the book. Anyway, if the novel is on an examination syllabus it goes without saying that it has something to recommend it.

Use of Quotations

We have talked earlier about quoting from *Of Mice and Men*. Have you considered reading about what Steinbeck said about the book, and quoting from him? Showing that you have done that amount of research could be the difference between a B grade and an A or A*. There are various quotations from Steinbeck in these York Notes. It is also possible to provide evidence for some themes by quoting from other novels by Steinbeck, though you should do this very sparingly.

CHECK THE BOOK

You can find quotations from Steinbeck in *Conversations with John Steinbeck* (University Press of Mississippi, 1988) and in *John Steinbeck: A Life in Letters* (Heinemann, 1975).

EXTRA KNOWLEDGE AND BACKGROUND READING

Most candidates for an examination will have read the set text. Many fewer will have read other books by the author, or books that throw light on the set text by other authors. You can have too much of a good thing – someone who has read widely round the subject can have a tendency to spend the whole answer writing about the other things they have read, and not about the set text – but you give yourself a head start over other candidates if you refer to wider reading in your answer. Apart from anything else, background reading always helps you to put the set text into perspective. The best books to read for someone studying *Of Mice and Men* are *The Grapes of Wrath*, *Tortilla Flat* and *Cannery Row*.

THE VARIETY OF POSSIBLE RESPONSES

One way to improve your grade is to realise that when you are studying a book there is no one viewpoint that is absolutely and totally right. A good, solid answer will deal with the **themes** that can be found in *Of Mice and Men*. The outstanding answer will argue passionately that one or two themes are dominant in the novel, but will never pretend that the other themes are not there.

A PERSONAL RESPONSE

The advice to be enthusiastic and passionate about what you have read is something that you will rarely find in study guides such as this. However, one of the best ways to improve your grade is to show that the novel has made you think and feel, and that you have been excited by it. We hope that York Notes will help you on your way to this sort of personal response.

CHECK THE FILM

Do the films match the vision you have in your head? Do the films merely seek to repeat in visual form what Steinbeck did in print? Or do the films go beyond what Steinbeck wrote?

SAMPLE ESSAY PLAN

A typical essay question on *Of Mice and Men* is followed by a sample essay plan in note form. This does not present the only answer to the question, merely one answer. Do not be afraid to include your own ideas, and leave out some of those in the sample! Remember that quotations are essential to prove and illustrate the points you make.

To what extent is *Of Mice and Men* a novel of protest?

INTRODUCTION

Steinbeck's most famous novel, *The Grapes of Wrath*, is a protest novel. But it is wrong to judge one novel on the basis of another.

PART 1

There is certainly much protest in the novel, against:

- The treatment of old people (Candy and dog)
- Racism (Crooks)
- Those who work land not reaping its rewards
- Loneliness (Candy, Crooks, George and Lennie)

CHECKPOINT 20

What is the difference between the words 'quote' and 'quotation'?

PART 2

There are some areas, however, where there is no protest at all:

- Against treatment of people with special needs (Lennie)
- No complaint against ranch owner: 'nice fella' (p. 22)
- Ranch hands seem to live quite well
- Against what George does to Lennie, just sad acceptance: 'You hadda, George' (p. 106)

PART 3

EXAMINER'S SECRET
Be absolutely relevant and answer the question at all times.

The label 'novel of protest' does not do justice to the book in terms of its:

- Compassion and care for individuals
- Grasp of the beauties of nature
- Treatment of people's need to dream
- Vision of freedom
- Treatment of the theme of loneliness

CONCLUSION

Of Mice and Men is a novel of compassion. It does not protest about life. It observes life and recreates it, leaving the reader to judge.

FURTHER QUESTIONS

Make a plan as shown above and attempt these questions:

EXAMINER'S SECRET
Don't change your mind about what you think the answer is halfway through an essay.

1 Are there any weaknesses in *Of Mice and Men*?

2 To what extent is Steinbeck's style 'dramatic' in *Of Mice and Men*?

3 What contribution does Slim make to *Of Mice and Men*?

4 Is *Of Mice and Men* a pessimistic novel?

5 Does Steinbeck condemn Curley's wife, or does he sympathise with her?

6 Why does George shoot Lennie?

7 What are the main techniques that Steinbeck uses to create atmosphere in *Of Mice and Men*?

8 How significant is the theme of loneliness in *Of Mice and Men*?

9 'There are too many disabilities, misfits and unusual characters in *Of Mice and Men* for it to be described accurately as true to life.' Discuss.

10 What is the importance of dreams and dreaming to the success of *Of Mice and Men*?

EXAMINER'S SECRET
Write a forceful opening and a conclusive ending.

Now take a break!

characterisation the techniques by which an author describes and tries to bring to life the characters in his or her work. There are as many variations in this as there are characters, and characterisation that is both convincing and realistic is essential to the success of any novel

dialogue the speech and conversation of characters in a novel, play or poem. Capturing the 'feel' of real speech is one of the hardest things a novelist has to do

image, imagery a word-picture that describes some scene, person or object. More often the term is used of similes or metaphors. Authors often draw their images from certain areas. Steinbeck favours natural imagery, and images based on light

irony saying one thing while meaning another. Crooks is being ironic when he says it is 'swell' (p. 74) to have a room with a manure heap outside the window

metaphor a description in which a person or object is described as being something else, as in the water-snake, 'twisting its periscope head' (p. 98)

motif a theme, character or image that recurs again and again in a novel or work of literature. The rabbits in Lennie's dreams and mind are a motif, running like a theme tune through the novel

myth/mythologising myth has two meanings. The common one of something that is untrue ('It is a myth that …') should not be confused with its literary meaning. A myth is a story often associated with religious beliefs, based on supernatural or god-like characters, and commenting on issues central to human existence. The central story of a myth can be adapted and rewritten to fit other times, and such famous works as Shelley's *Prometheus Unbound* (1820) or J.R.R. Tolkien's *The Lord of the Rings* (1954–55) rework one or more established myths. An author can, of course, attempt to create a myth as well as to use an existing one

paradox usually an apparent contradiction that on closer examination turns out not to be a contradiction at all. It usually relies on placing two opposites alongside each other

simile a description in which a person or object is described as being as or like something else, as in, 'little rolled clusters, like sausages' (p. 32)

symbol an image that describes far more than the physical features of the object described. The heron that kills the water-snake is a physical object but it is also a symbol of nature, telling you what it stands for and what it contains

theme central idea or ideas that are examined with a view to some serious questions being asked, and some conclusions being drawn; the overriding topic or topics that interest a writer in his book. Loneliness is a theme in *Of Mice and Men*

CHECKPOINT 1 The only animal that plays a real part in the novel is Candy's dog.

CHECKPOINT 2 George probably knows the dream will never be realised, but protects himself and Lennie by clinging to the hope that it will happen.

CHECKPOINT 3 It is about everyone who is crushed by society.

CHECKPOINT 4 a bear; a terrier; a cuckoo

CHECKPOINT 5 Lennie appears as a 'gentle giant' because he never means the hurt he causes, and quite literally he does not know the extent of his own strength.

CHECKPOINT 6 We learn that it is plain, functional, and impersonal, somewhere through which large numbers of men pass leaving no permanent mark.

CHECKPOINT 7 George's physical cleanliness is emphasised by his concern over lice in his bunk, his mental cleanliness by rejection of the whorehouse.

CHECKPOINT 8 Well over half the novel is written in dialogue, and much of the characterisation is achieved by the tone and content of the characters' speech.

CHECKPOINT 9 We learn that Lennie clung on to a girl's dress, that she accused him of rape and that Lennie only survived because of George.

CHECKPOINT 10 Any magazine that offers an escape from people bored with their lives.

CHECKPOINT 11 A large number of hints as to a tragic ending are given, such as the death of the animals Lennie keeps and Lennie's own cry, 'This ain't no good place' (p. 34).

CHECKPOINT 12 Yes, we are meant to sympathise with and even like her a little. She is a victim, as are so many other people in the novel.

CHECKPOINT 13 It would not be as effective for Lennie to be associated with children because children have the capacity to grow up, and we know that Lennie will never grow up.

CHECKPOINT 14 The lines are possibly too poetic, but it could be that they are even stronger by being unusual.

CHECKPOINT 15 Lennie's dream visions can be unconvincing, but the killing of Lennie is told effectively.

CHECKPOINT 16 Slim is correct. The alternative would be a lingering legalised death for Lennie at the hands of those who did not love him.

CHECKPOINT 17 From what we know about the economic climate of the times, no. If the smallholding is profitable, why is it for sale so cheaply?

CHECKPOINT 18 The pessimistic part of the novel is that hope is dashed. The optimistic part is that it exists in the first place.

CHECKPOINT 19 For example: Laurel and Hardy; Morecombe and Wise; Little and Large

CHECKPOINT 20 A quotation is an extract from a work, and is a noun. 'To quote' is a verb, and you should never refer to 'a quote', but always 'a quotation'.

TEST YOURSELF (PAGES 3–18)

1 George *(p. 8)*

2 Lennie *(p. 8)*

3 Lennie *(p. 11)*

4 George *(p.12)*

5 George *(p. 16)*

6 Bus driver *(p. 6)*

7 Aunt Clara *(p. 11)*

TEST YOURSELF (PAGES 19–38)

1 Curley *(p. 38)*

2 Candy *(p. 26)*

3 Carlson *(p. 37)*

4 Slim *(p. 36)*

5 Lennie *(p. 34)*

6 The boss *(p. 22)*

7 Curley *(p. 28)*

8 Slim *(p. 35)*

TEST YOURSELF (PAGES 39–65)

1 George *(p. 41)*

2 Carlson *(p. 48)*

3 George *(p. 41)*

4 Candy *(p. 60)*

5 Curley *(p. 62)*

6 Lennie *(p. 40)*

7 Lennie *(p. 44)*

8 Curley *(p. 64)*

9 Lennie *(p. 59)*

TEST YOURSELF (PAGES 66–82)

1 Crooks *(p. 71)*

2 Candy *(p. 75)*

3 Curley's wife *(p. 77)*

4 Crooks *(p. 73)*

5 Crooks *(p. 68)*

6 Curley's wife *(p. 79)*

7 Curley *(p.77)*

8 Crooks *(p. 67)*

TEST YOURSELF (PAGES 83–97)

1 Candy *(p. 93)*

2 Lennie *(p. 84)*

3 Curley's wife *(p. 85)*

4 George *(p. 94)*

5 Lennie *(p. 88)*

6 Curley's wife *(p. 91)*

7 Curley *(p. 87)*

8 Candy *(p. 92)*

TEST YOURSELF (PAGES 98–106)

1 Lennie *(p. 103)*

2 George *(p. 104)*

3 vision of Aunt Clara in Lennie's voice *(p. 100)*

4 Slim *(p. 106)*

5 Lennie *(p. 102)*

6 George and Slim *(p. 106)*

7 Lennie *(p. 98)*

8 George *(p. 105)*

NOTES

Maya Angelou
I Know Why the Caged Bird Sings

Jane Austen
Pride and Prejudice

Alan Ayckbourn
Absent Friends

Elizabeth Barrett Browning
Selected Poems

Robert Bolt
A Man for All Seasons

Harold Brighouse
Hobson's Choice

Charlotte Brontë
Jane Eyre

Emily Brontë
Wuthering Heights

Shelagh Delaney
A Taste of Honey

Charles Dickens
David Copperfield
Great Expectations
Hard Times
Oliver Twist

Roddy Doyle
Paddy Clarke Ha Ha Ha

George Eliot
Silas Marner
The Mill on the Floss

Anne Frank
The Diary of a Young Girl

William Golding
Lord of the Flies

Oliver Goldsmith
She Stoops to Conquer

Willis Hall
The Long and the Short and the Tall

Thomas Hardy
Far from the Madding Crowd

The Mayor of Casterbridge
Tess of the d'Urbervilles
The Withered Arm and other Wessex Tales

L.P. Hartley
The Go-Between

Seamus Heaney
Selected Poems

Susan Hill
I'm the King of the Castle

Barry Hines
A Kestrel for a Knave

Louise Lawrence
Children of the Dust

Harper Lee
To Kill a Mockingbird

Laurie Lee
Cider with Rosie

Arthur Miller
The Crucible
A View from the Bridge

Robert O'Brien
Z for Zachariah

Frank O'Connor
My Oedipus Complex and Other Stories

George Orwell
Animal Farm

J.B. Priestley
An Inspector Calls
When We Are Married

Willy Russell
Educating Rita
Our Day Out

J.D. Salinger
The Catcher in the Rye

William Shakespeare
Henry IV Part 1
Henry V
Julius Caesar

Macbeth
The Merchant of Venice
A Midsummer Night's Dream
Much Ado About Nothing
Romeo and Juliet
The Tempest
Twelfth Night

George Bernard Shaw
Pygmalion

Mary Shelley
Frankenstein

R.C. Sherriff
Journey's End

Rukshana Smith
Salt on the snow

John Steinbeck
Of Mice and Men

Robert Louis Stevenson
Dr Jekyll and Mr Hyde

Jonathan Swift
Gulliver's Travels

Robert Swindells
Daz 4 Zoe

Mildred D. Taylor
Roll of Thunder, Hear My Cry

Mark Twain
Huckleberry Finn

James Watson
Talking in Whispers

Edith Wharton
Ethan Frome

William Wordsworth
Selected Poems

A Choice of Poets
Mystery Stories of the Nineteenth Century including The Signalman
Nineteenth Century Short Stories
Poetry of the First World War
Six Women Poets

Margaret Atwood
Cat's Eye
The Handmaid's Tale

Jane Austen
Emma
Mansfield Park
Persuasion
Pride and Prejudice
Sense and Sensibility

Alan Bennett
Talking Heads

William Blake
*Songs of Innocence and of
Experience*

Charlotte Brontë
Jane Eyre
Villette

Emily Brontë
Wuthering Heights

Angela Carter
Nights at the Circus

Geoffrey Chaucer
The Franklin's Prologue and Tale
The Miller's Prologue and Tale
*The Prologue to the Canterbury
Tales*
*The Wife of Bath's Prologue and
Tale*

Samuel Coleridge
Selected Poems

Joseph Conrad
Heart of Darkness

Daniel Defoe
Moll Flanders

Charles Dickens
Bleak House
Great Expectations
Hard Times

Emily Dickinson
Selected Poems

John Donne
Selected Poems

Carol Ann Duffy
Selected Poems

George Eliot
Middlemarch
The Mill on the Floss

T.S. Eliot
Selected Poems
The Waste Land

F. Scott Fitzgerald
The Great Gatsby

E.M. Forster
A Passage to India

Brian Friel
Translations

Thomas Hardy
Jude the Obscure
The Mayor of Casterbridge
The Return of the Native
Selected Poems
Tess of the d'Urbervilles

Seamus Heaney
*Selected Poems from 'Opened
Ground'*

Nathaniel Hawthorne
The Scarlet Letter

Homer
The Iliad
The Odyssey

Aldous Huxley
Brave New World

Kazuo Ishiguro
The Remains of the Day

Ben Jonson
The Alchemist

James Joyce
Dubliners

John Keats
Selected Poems

Christopher Marlowe
Doctor Faustus
Edward II

Arthur Miller
Death of a Salesman

John Milton
Paradise Lost Books I & II

Toni Morrison
Beloved

George Orwell
Nineteen Eighty-Four

Sylvia Plath
Selected Poems

Alexander Pope
*Rape of the Lock & Selected
Poems*

William Shakespeare
Antony and Cleopatra
As You Like It
Hamlet
Henry IV Part I
King Lear
Macbeth
Measure for Measure
The Merchant of Venice
A Midsummer Night's Dream
Much Ado About Nothing
Othello
Richard II
Richard III
Romeo and Juliet
The Taming of the Shrew
The Tempest
Twelfth Night
The Winter's Tale

George Bernard Shaw
Saint Joan

Mary Shelley
Frankenstein

Jonathan Swift
*Gulliver's Travels and A Modest
Proposal*

Alfred Tennyson
Selected Poems

Virgil
The Aeneid

Alice Walker
The Color Purple

Oscar Wilde
The Importance of Being Earnest

Tennessee Williams
A Streetcar Named Desire

Jeanette Winterson
Oranges Are Not the Only Fruit

John Webster
The Duchess of Malfi

Virginia Woolf
To the Lighthouse

W.B. Yeats
Selected Poems

Metaphysical Poets

The Ultimate Web Site for the Ultimate Literature Guides

At York Notes we believe in helping you achieve exam success. Log on to **www.yorknotes.com** and see how we have made revision even easier, with over 300 titles available to download twenty-four hours a day. The downloads have lots of additional features such as pop-up boxes providing instant glossary definitions, user-friendly links to every part of the guide, and scanned illustrations offering visual appeal. All you need to do is log on to **www.yorknotes.com** and download the books you need to help you achieve exam success.

Key Features:

Details on how York Notes can help you

Menu Bar to help you find your way around the site

Details on how to download York Notes

Quick Search facility to help you find the titles you need

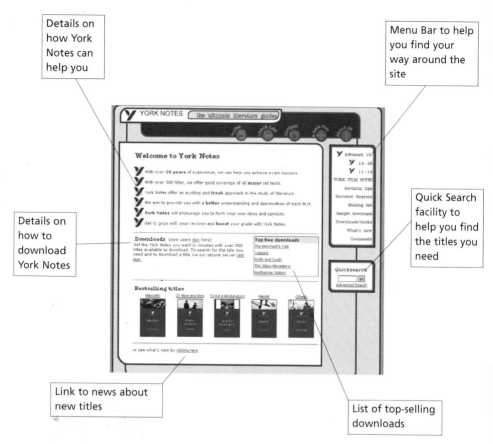

Link to news about new titles

List of top-selling downloads